DATE DUE

APR 24 '71	MAR 18 '73	OCT 15 '83
	AUG 13 '73	U. C.
MAY 10 '71	M. H. C.	MAR 23 '85
	MAY 6 '74	OCT 25 '92
AUG 16 '71	JUL 12 '74	NOV 17 '92
OCT 16 '71	NOV 8 '74	MAR 14 2002
	DEC 14 '74	
NOV 8 '71 DEC 13 '71	AUG 14 '75	
APR 15 '72	MAR 20 '76	
MAY 8 '72	MAY 1 '76	
JUN 19 '72	DEC 10 '77	
JUL 14 '72	DEC 15 '79	
FEB 17 '73	MAY 31 '82	

GAYLORD   PRINTED IN U.S.A.

SPECIAL EDUCATION
IN THE REGULAR CLASSROOM

SPECIAL EDUCATION IN THE REGULAR CLASSROOM

ERNEST SIEGEL, Ed. D.

Supervisor, Education of the Physically Handicapped
New York City Board of Education

THE JOHN DAY COMPANY, NEW YORK

Copyright © 1969 by Ernest Siegel

All rights reserved. No part of this book may be reprinted, or reproduced or utilized in any form or by any electronic, mechanical or other means, now known or hereafter invented, including photocopying and recording, or in any information storage and retrieval system, without permission in writing from the Publisher, The John Day Company, Inc., 62 West 45th Street, New York, N.Y. 10036. Published on the same day in Canada by Longmans Canada Limited.

Library of Congress Catalogue Card Number: 75-79713

PRINTED IN THE UNITED STATES OF AMERICA

Acknowledgments

My sincere appreciation to all who have encouraged, assisted, and supported me in the completion of this project:

To Mortimer Kreuter, assistant director of the Center for Urban Education, New York City, for his genuine concern with the plight of the exceptional child in the regular classroom and for his confidence in me, personally. He was certainly an original source of inspiration, having become interested in this book at its very inception.

To the many individuals who, upon either reading portions of the manuscript or hearing my accounts of several sections, offered their assurances that a book devoted to this topic could make a genuine contribution. These include Manfred F. Drewski, consultant in special education, Department of Education of New Hampshire; John Gulian, co-director of the Great Bay Training Center, Newington, New Hampshire; Stanley Eaton, chairman (1966), school psychologists section of the Western Zone Teachers Conference, New York; Ben Brooks, Special Education Fellow, University of New Mexico, and Walter A. Kelly, director of special education, Archdiocese of New York.

To Shirley Greenwald, guidance consultant for the physically handicapped, New York City Board of Education, for her critical review of several sections. Her opinions were most valuable.

To the students in my various college courses for their willingness to share their experiences, needs, and ideas with me, thereby strengthening—and, at times, modifying—some of my opinions.

To the Center for Urban Education of New York City for sponsoring an all-day conference on June 1, 1966, devoted to the topic of special education in the regular classroom. I am grateful to Marcus Arnold, director of the Bureau for Education of Physically Handicapped, New York City Board of Education, for addressing this conference and for arranging for many of the participants to attend.

To Lee Lewin of the Adams School, New York City, for her encouragement and for bringing the author and publisher together.

To the various publishers who graciously permitted the quoting of portions of their publications.

To the librarians, for their cooperation, especially those of the professional library of New York City Board of Education, and of the Academy of Medicine of New York City.

To Martha Bryant, administrative secretary of the Center for Urban Education, New York City, for her interest in this project and for typing portions of the manuscript.

And, of course, I am genuinely grateful to my wife, Rita, for typing, proofreading, and editing; for her many valuable suggestions (she is a teacher as well as a mother); and for her unwavering faith in me. Finally, allow me to thank and sympathize with my sons—Phillip, Paul, and Peter—for the many hours in which they had to "play quietly."

Preface

I first met Dr. Ernest Siegel about ten years ago when we were both teaching in the graduate teacher education program at a large city university. One night we decided to combine classes so that our students could benefit from hearing different viewpoints. The great breadth of Siegel's grasp of the clinical and psychological principles underlying special education became apparent. Particularly impressive was his ability to answer specific questions related to children's discrepant development and how learning theories could be applied to recurrent classroom demands. Over the ensuing years, I have had occasion to meet with hundreds of teachers and to utilize many of the practical suggestions I learned from a close working relationship with Ernest Siegel. Ernest was among the first of the special education leaders to stay closely related to the perennial questions of the regular teacher, of what to do with the handicapped child—whether perceptually or behaviorally or intellectually impaired—found in every school. Therefore, it was with a great deal of pleasure that I learned of the preparation of this book and reading it has confirmed my anticipation.

Special Education in the Regular Classroom appears at a fortuitous time, for it has been during the decade of the sixties that American educators have turned their attention increasingly to the learning needs of handicapped children. As our understanding of the rights of individuals to the fullest pursuit of the good life broadens and deepens, we are opening wider the schoolhouse door to the child with severe emotional handicaps, once excluded because of, in the quaint words of one state's educational law, "unamenability to instruction." As our social conscience quickens to the academic plight of socially segregated and economically deprived urban youngsters, we develop a system of federal supports to aid in the remedial and instructional processes and there appears to be no question any longer in this country of excluding from school even the most barely intellectually capable or the most sorely neglected child. During this time of educational crisis, the marvelously robust American characteristic of making anything operate efficiently and of being able to overcome all social odds for improving every child's life chances is reemerging throughout the country's schools, especially with regard to children with learning problems. School systems are taking on, and in some cases actively seeking out, all kinds of learners. In this social engagement, we seem to be saying that we can do more than any country has ever done for the handicapped in all recorded history. There is an enormous expansion of special education everywhere one looks, and the need for new methods and materials for instructing the handicapped is great.

At the same time, reputable educators concerned with the needs of handicapped children have been expressing some doubts as to the reliability and validity of the special class treatment for many of these children. This is particularly true in relation to those who are minimally handicapped. For many reasons it is strongly believed that there are better ways of serving these children than placing them in self-contained special schools or classes. This latter organization often serves not only as a deterrent to these children returning to the mainstream of education or in assuming a productive role in society but often results in a permanent disability label because of inadequate assessment. Such a disability label is not only not needed; it helps to fulfill prophecies of inadequacy or failure even where they never were quite spelled out to begin with. Rather, the needed educational help should be recognized and a stimulating setting for individual growth and development be planned and fostered in the regular classroom so that the immersion of the handicapped in the total process of education will eventually fortify such persons for living in the normal world.

Through segregation and "special" treatment, certain values and attitudes are perpetuated which could disfavor a group considered to be school retardates. Deeper knowledge and greater insight concerning the needs of these handicapped children have been a by-product of various programs attempted within the past few years. Such organizational patterns as prekindergarten programs, team teaching, and smaller ratio of children to teachers have offered opportunities to observe the disabilities of children and to discover a variety of methods in diminishing them. These treatments focus on modifications in curriculum that recognize the actual needs of children, and they serve to influence the disappearance of the specious and disparaging separation of these children from the mainstream of school life. Special organization will still be available for distinctively impaired children. However, those children who may be judged to have mild learning disorders may be better served within the regular classroom, provided that the classroom teacher is aware of the modifications that will be most fitting and supportive. The children included in the regular classroom will find security in the readiness of the teacher to accept their individual disabilities and in the creativity with which the teacher seeks those techniques and materials for guided instruction that will lessen these disabilities and help them meet success academically.

It is for the express purpose of preparing educators to work productively with the untold numbers of minimally handicapped children in the regular classes that Dr. Ernest Siegel has prepared this volume. Himself a veteran of more than twenty years' experience as an educator, writer, and clinician with the neurologically impaired child with severe learning deficits, Siegel recognizes that no matter how great our efforts at providing special facilities for the severely handicapped school-age child, we shall always have enormous numbers of children with not so easily detected learning problems in regular classes. In his *Special Education in the Regular Classroom,* Siegel, through a variety of concrete examples and techniques drawn from the relevant literature and tested against his own richly stocked background in individualized instruction of the handicapped, has crafted a work of immense value to classroom teachers.

Dr. Siegel asks, "What is special education?" Does the reply have to refer to special, segregated classes or schools? In his view, the approach to children selectively and deliberately as well as in group considerations can make up a "special education." The teacher looks at each child as a special individual and proceeds to look for the key to understanding. What is it that will turn each child on? What is it that each child needs? What is his self-image? In his review of the literature in the field, Dr. Siegel specifically annotates that special education need not necessarily mean a form of apartheid education but that special education will occur in the regular classroom when the exceptional child is there and teachers make specific efforts to teach him.

Siegel presents a functional curriculum approach for educating the minimally handicapped child with major emphasis on how and why to modify specific, definite learning experiences. He has particularly selected those population entities which include only those children suffering from learning and/or behavioral disorders as a basis for presenting his carefully considered ideas. The medically and psychologically oriented entities of mental retardation, brain impairment, and emotional disturbance serve as valuable illustrations. The teacher who feels a commitment to helping children with some mild form of these conditions will find valuable guidance in the methods or approaches, as they are herein described, to meet a specific learning or a moment when some behavioral problems are involved. Such help is offered by the author, who has examined the three populations as having many areas of commonalities. His suggestions, presented in a variety of exercises for teaching children with specific learning difficulties, imply the necessity for the teacher to assess the learning potential of each child. As the teacher does this for those few children in the class, he gains greater insight into the other children as well. Indeed, as the indicated methods offer special direction in meeting success in organizing things, in cognitive growth, and in oral language development among a vast variety of class experiences, there should be noted an effect upon the efforts of the other children. With no equivocation, it can easily be seen how the self-image of the handicapped children can assume an affirmative form by being in itself an example to their nonhandicapped classmates of how a teacher's interest and their own application helped them to learn adequately.

This book is addressed to the teacher of a regular classroom. It does concern a challenge, but it will help the regular teacher by offering information about symptoms that are observable, sometimes the causes for them, and proposed treatment of the child's difficulties. The teacher will be able to recognize and identify the three specific types of exceptionality and will be prepared to help in the total development of the handicapped child by being ready to take the necessary action. Since much of the implementation of a program for the education of these handicapped children is the responsibility of the teacher, the contents of this book will not only help orient the teacher in a direct manner to the child's disabilities but will also serve as a continuous resource for ongoing training. By going where the action is, the regular classroom, and by focusing his attention on the teaching-learning process for the mildly handicapped child, Dr. Ernest Siegel has restored to the teacher the most powerful of her techniques: diagnosis followed by carefully prescribed and personalized instruction. In doing so, he has made an inestimable contribution to the fields of education, guidance, school psychology, and school administration, the practitioners of which can make use of the materials presented with children, teachers, parents, and others concerned with the handicapped child.

>MORTIMER KREUTER
>Assistant Director, Center for Urban Education
>   and
>Associate Professor of Special Education
>Teachers College, Columbia University

Contents

Acknowledgments	v
Preface	vii
Foreword	xv

1. Introduction — 1
    What Is Special Education? — 1
    Unique Problems of the Mildly Handicapped Child — 4
    References — 10

2. The Exceptional Child — 13
    The Mentally Retarded Child — 15
    The Brain-Injured Child — 19
    The Emotionally Disturbed Child — 28
    References — 40

3. The Teacher's Role: Techniques for Solving Nine Basic Problems — 44
    Poor Self-Concept — 46
    Anxiety — 50

	Difficulty in Paying Attention	55
	Difficulty in Organizing	63
	Difficulty in Copying Written Material	65
	Poor Coordination	68
	Difficulty in Abstract Thinking	75
	Behavioral Problems	84
	Social Immaturity	93
	References	103
4.	**Additional Aspects of the Teacher's Role**	108
	Assisting in Identification	108
	Gathering and Sharing Information	112
	Utilizing Supportive Services	113
	Participation in In-Service Training	116
	Lesson Planning	119
	Relationships with Parents	121
	References	126
5.	**The Role of the School Administrator**	128
	Supporting the Teacher	129
	Supporting the Child	132
	Supporting the Program	136
	Working with the Community	139
	References	142
6.	**The Role of Teacher-Training Institutions**	143
	Teacher Preparation	143
	Working with the Community	149
	Research	150
	References	151
	Bibliography	153
	Index	163

Foreword

Texts and courses in special education are almost entirely geared toward special classes. There is very little emphasis on helping the marginally exceptional child in the regular classroom; these children, however, are enrolled (and in considerable number) in regular classrooms throughout the country.

Educators differ in their opinions as to who is the recipient of the majority of public educational services. Some staunchly maintain that education, generally, is suited to the needs of the average child and that the children with special needs go by the wayside.

"Not so," argues another group of educators. "Just witness the rise in facilities for exceptional children, and you must agree that it is the average child who is discriminated against."

There is some validity in both opinions. Education, by and large, is geared to the normal child, but superimposed upon this picture is the accelerated pace with which public school systems are making provisions for the exceptional child in special classes.

The truly neglected group of children, however, remains the *marginally* exceptional—those who are neither significantly "exceptional" to warrant special placement nor sufficiently "normal" to benefit from regular classroom placement *without proper orientation on the part of the teacher and other school personnel.*

SPECIAL EDUCATION
IN THE REGULAR CLASSROOM

CHAPTER

1

Introduction

What Is Special Education?

There is a paradox inherent in the term special education. As we establish more and more classes for exceptional children and as we differentiate more and more clearly the teacher-training requirements of the special class teacher from the regular class teacher, the exceptional children tend to represent a unique group, apart and distinct from normal children. Moreover, there is a tendency to feel that their needs can best be met in these special classes. There is even a semantic logic to this feeling: Who can dispute the soundness of the motto "special classes for special children"? From this philosophy, there is only a short bridge to the notion that exceptional children's needs cannot be met in regular classes. This does not necessarily follow, and herein lies the paradox: (1) In our efforts to help exceptional children, we set up more special facilities for them. (2) In so doing, we draw a line of demarcation between special education and regular education. (3) The very child that we wish to help might under certain circumstances best be helped in a regular classroom, but our educational apartheid policy affecting teacher-training institutions, public school administration and the orientation of regular classroom teachers militate against this child's attaining his potential.

Definitions of "exceptional children" and of "special education" have, in the main, been somewhat circular—one explaining the other. Kirk (1950: 3) defined exceptional children as, "those . . . who deviate from what is supposed to be average in physical, mental, emotional, or social characteristics to such an extent that they require special educational services in order to develop to their maximum capacity. . . ." This definition was repeated by Baker (1959: 11), Cruickshank (1958: 3) and Dunn (1963: 44).

Kirk (1962: 32) regarded "special education" as "that additional education service over and above the regular school program, which is provided for an exceptional child to assist in the development of his potentialities. . . ." Dunn's (1963: 3) definition of "special education" was quite specific, stipulating three differentiating elements: specially trained professional personnel, special curricular content and special facilities.

Many writers, however, while endorsing the symbiotic definitions of "exceptional children" and "special education" (*i.e.,* exceptional children are those who need special education, and special education is that educational program which can help the exceptional child reach his potential) do state, or rather concede, that special education can occur in a regular classroom. For example, Kirk (1962: 5) stated that the exceptional child needs special education "either in conjunction with a regular class or in a special class. . . ." Cruickshank (1958: 20–21) believed that "not all exceptional children need special education. Some children may simply require modification in their regular classroom or program." Wooden (1953: 179) also believed that "not all exceptional children need special education—and many who need it for a time do not need it indefinitely. . . . [an exceptional child] may make, under *favorable* conditions, a reasonably good adjustment in regular classroom." Kirk (1950: 3) states that the special education that an exceptional child needs can "sometimes be offered best through the medium of a special class or school; but, in many cases, they may be provided for individual pupils in a regular class. . . ."

Wooden (1953: 179) considered the crucial factor separating special education from regular education to be training of the special teacher: "Special education . . . is provision for those individual differences among children for which regular teachers are not trained and for which they therefore do not possess competence and skill. . . ." Blackman and Sparks (1965: 242–43) pointed out: "An assumption underlying the placement of educable mentally retarded children in special classes and in the special preparation of the teachers is that the special teachers require instructional skills not normally required of teachers of the regular grades."

Despite this feeling that special class teachers are, by virtue of their training, better equipped to help the exceptional child than are the regular class teachers, the fact remains that many exceptional children are enrolled in regular classes (Dunn 1963: 111; Bower 1957). This may be related to a large extent to the perennial shortage of special teachers. Even with the colleges' and universities' post–World War II interest in and expansion of their special teacher education programs, it is unlikely that the gap between supply and demand will be eliminated (Cruickshank 1958: 25–28). The presence of handicapped children in regular classes may also be the result of the philosophy of integrating students whenever possible. Still another reason is the administrative difficulty of establishing special classes for handicapped children who are "spread out" in sparsely populated rural areas. But whatever the reasons, the fact is that exceptional children *are* enrolled in regular classes. As Dolch (1948: v–vi) predicted: "For a long time, the regular teacher will carry the burden of educating the handicapped. She must know as much as she can about the difficulties so that she may do what she can. . . . [She must know] how to identify the handicapped, how to understand his difficulties and how to help him under school conditions. . . ."

In essence, then, the following points should be noted:

1. By definition as well as by philosophy "special education" can be undertaken in a regular classroom.
2. Many handicapped children are enrolled in regular classrooms.
3. "Under certain conditions" and with some "modification," the exceptional child can be helped best in a regular classroom.

It is to this third point that we address ourselves. The purpose of this book is to suggest, to explore and to stipulate these "certain conditions" and "modifications"—to put into the hands of classroom teachers and principals some specific suggestions for increasing the mildly handicapped child's school achievement and adjustment.

Unique Problems of the Mildly Handicapped Child

The emphasis of this book is on the *minimally* handicapped child in the regular classroom; however, it should be pointed out that at times regular school programs have enrolled even the *more seriously* handicapped in classes with nonhandicapped children, including various areas of exceptionality such as the orthopedically handicapped (Connor 1958: 447; Bowden and Otto 1964), the blind (Gray 1956), the epileptic (Tenny and Lenox 1951) and the mentally retarded (Blackman n.d.). In many of these programs it is the *intention* of the educators to include these severely handicapped individuals in regular classes; in other instances it happens fortuitously. This is especially true in the case of emotionally disturbed children, where the severity of the disability is seldom discovered in the doctor's office but generally is first diagnosed in the classroom (Long and Newman 1961: 313).

Now, if the regular classrooms contain *some* severely handicapped children, it becomes apparent that they must contain *many* (at least, by comparison) minimally handicapped. These children are handicapped by the very mildness of their condition as well as by the actual limitations resulting from their medical and/or pyschological disabilities.

It seems obvious to both professionals and laymen that a severely disabled child has more problems than does a child who is less disabled. After all, are the blind not far more burdened than the partially sighted? Is not the nonambulatory orthopedic more unfortunate than the child with a mild limp? Do the deaf not find themselves deprived of more of their environment than those with a slight hearing loss? Surprisingly, research has not always shown a 100 percent positive correlation between severity of physical disability and severity of resultant educational, social or vocational problems. As a matter of fact, sometimes the contrary is true. For example, in a study involving cerebral palsied adults (Glick 1963: 240–41) it was found that only 7 percent of the mildly disabled group were employed, whereas 22 percent of the moderately disabled and 24 percent of the severely disabled were able to hold jobs; the discrepancy was explained on the basis of inability of the mildly disabled group to get along with fellow employees. Sensory deprivation studies (Freedman, Grunebaum and Greenblatt 1961: 58–71) show poorer performance (*e.g.*, perceptual distortion, deterioration of form-quality on Bender Motor Gestalt Tests, less improvement in rotary-pursuit tasks, etc.) for those subjects who received unpatterned sensory stimulation than for those who underwent total deprivation. Heider (Magary and Eichorn 1962: 307–8), in contrasting a totally deaf child with one having partial hearing, explains: "If he were wholly cut off, the situation would not be so tantalizing as that in which he finds himself, where he can understand part of a conversation and then perhaps lose just the key word that explains everything. The boundaries between what he can do and cannot do are not clearly defined and from this point of view his whole life situation is poorly structured. . . ." Strauss and Kephart (1955: 206) emphasize this point in terms of compensatory mechanisms:

One paradoxical fact needs special mention. A major damage involving gross interference with function is frequently less disturbing than a minor damage which interferes only slightly. In the case of a major damage the disturbance is so gross that it is relatively easy to recognize and the individual develops compensatory activities which permit him to operate effectively without the necessity of using the damaged area. If, however, the damage is slight, its effects are not so easily recognized. The result is that a large number of activities are disturbed slightly, so little that the individual cannot recognize the disturbance. He therefore cannot develop the compensating activities which would allow him to operate, because he cannot locate the focal point of the difficulty.

All this is not to say that the problems facing the handicapped child are not dependent both in quantity and severity upon the degree of disability. Nevertheless, the mildly handicapped child has some problems that escape his more severely handicapped counterpart—they are different *kinds* of problems —they are the unique problems which exist by virtue of the very "minimal" nature of the condition (Siegel 1961: 43).

DIFFICULTY IN DIAGNOSING. Generally speaking, the greater the handicap, the greater the chances for diagnosis. Minimal injuries may reveal themselves only as situations and requirements develop (Taft n.d.). Hence, a child with neurological impairment may not appear to be handicapped until he reaches the age at which he is supposed to learn to walk. A mildly retarded child might seem completely normal from birth through kindergarten, and not appear as deviant until he encounters the academic demands of first grade.

Even when the deviation does appear, it may be so slight as not to warrant any constructive concern. This, of course, is related to the insight, perceptiveness and tolerance level of the parent (and the teacher). On the whole, one seeks medical or psychological diagnosis only when the child is viewed as possessing significant problems. Hence, the capacity for tolerating a mildly handicapped child (*e.g.*, not recognizing his handicap), while an admirable trait from a standpoint of good mental hygiene, can actually militate against the child's well-being to the extent that it separates him from a diagnosis. Myklebust (1954: 1–2) says that a "child with impaired hearing acuity who is erroneously diagnosed as mentally deficient, aphasic, or emotionally disturbed suffers greatly, not only from his deafness, but from being misunderstood. *Inadequate diagnosis, treatment, and psychological management in early life often cause problems of intense magnitude in later life* [italics added]."

If *mis*diagnosis can be harmful, so can *non*diagnosis. Gesell and Amatruda (1941: 239) point out that "the child with a selective injury is usually so obviously handicapped that sympathetic understanding of his difficulties is a natural consequence. The child with only a minimal injury needs the very same recognition and understanding, and he too needs more than ordinary protection from stress and competition. . . ."

An important factor in determining whether a mildly handicapped child receives a diagnosis is the attitude of the parents. Some parents, not possessing the psychological strength to face reality, refuse to believe what they see or settle for an "underdiagnosis." They will think of their child as "a little slow" or "a bit nervous" but will not seek further scientific probings. It is as though they make a pact with themselves: "I do not recognize the problem; therefore it does not exist."

Finally, difficulties exist even when the child is brought in for examination. For example, minimal brain damage can often pass undetected on a neurological examination (Strauss and Lehtinen 1947: 106–12).

If a child has a mild, yet significant disability, it is undoubtedly to his advantage to obtain a diagnosis of it. Diagnoses are not sought merely to satisfy some whim or curiosity. Exceptional children can generally be treated more effectively in the early stages (Rimmele 1967: 89; Mase 1956: 341) and will more readily attain their optimum at maturity if they receive proper education and treatment services at the earliest possible time (Cruickshank 1958: 96).

Early diagnosis can facilitate the parents' understanding of the child and can help them relate to him in a more effective manner at a time when he needs this most. It can point the way toward parent orientation, adjustment and even parent counseling. For example, parents of a child with an undiagnosed hearing loss may reject the child for his nonresponsiveness. However, were the hearing loss detected at an early age, the parents could have been guided toward understanding and acceptance; moreover they could have been instructed in making specific modifications: *e.g.,* talking in sentences when sentences are normally used; talking in unexaggerated speech movements and in conversational tones; making sure the speaker's face is visible to the child, etc. (Roach 1962: 298–99).

FRUSTRATION. The mildly handicapped child usually engages in experiences alongside the normal child—that is, the child with no handicap. These experiences are largely competitive in nature, inasmuch as our society places so great a premium on achievement. Child and Bacon (1955: 168–69) point out that

> [The] degree of stress upon achievement in our own child training is very high indeed. This might be most strikingly illustrated by the fact that achievement pressures are in a sense exerted even at an age when they cannot possibly have an effect, as in praising a young baby for his birth weight or his liveliness. . . . Mothers in the park compete over teething schedules, time of rolling over, sitting up, smiling, etc. and anxiously consult publications which give developmental norms. . . . With the beginning of school, the pressure for achievement becomes more serious and is brought to bear more directly on the child. Children are divided into several reading groups according to their speed of learning. Stars are given for excellence of performance. Papers are graded on a scale of perfection, and marks are sent

home on a card at regular intervals. As children progress through school, the emphasis on achievement becomes more elaborate ... penetrates the area of recreation. There are real rewards for the child who shows athletic prowess. There is competition for the leading role in dramatic productions. Status in the Boy Scouts is definitely a function of various forms of achievement. There are even prizes for pinning the tail on a donkey at birthday parties.*

Feelings of frustration are, at the least, somewhat unpleasant, and at most they can be completely debilitating. Repetitive frustrations produce anxiety and negative self-concepts, which in turn can lead to inadequate performance, inappropriate coping mechanisms and peer rejection.

AMBIGUITY OF STATUS. Because of the "in between-ness" of his status, the minimally handicapped child often finds that he does not develop a true sense of belonging. He mingles with the unhandicapped children, but is he really one of them? At other times he is grouped with those more handicapped than himself, but does he identify with them? Those who work with him are equally perplexed. If the handicap is exaggerated, there can be a tendency to let him coast ("After all, he *is* handicapped, and we can't expect more of him."). On the other hand, if his medical or psychological disabilities are completely disregarded, one runs the risk of pushing beyond limits and placing the blame for all failure on volition ("Come on. You can do this if only you would try.").

LACK OF SYMPATHY AND UNDERSTANDING. One frequently hears spokesmen of the handicapped proclaiming, "We don't want sympathy; we want jobs." There can indeed be valid reasons for this feeling. "Sympathy" may contain such contaminating agents as devaluation, self-aggrandizement and insincerity (Wright 1960: 233–34). It may, however, be that the more severely handicapped child, surfeited with sympathy—

* Reprinted with permission from *Psychopathology of Childhood,* eds. Paul H. Hoch and Joseph Zubin (New York, Grune & Stratton, 1955).

even though it is genuine sympathy—no longer feels the need for this constant reassurance of tolerance and even of understanding. On the other hand, the mildly handicapped, appearing "normal," do not often evoke feelings of compassion in others. In fact, their inability to perform (learn, behave, communicate, work, socialize, etc.) at a level at least consistent with that of the statistical average often brings frowns, impatience and rejection—the implication being that the unsatisfactory performance is due to willfulness or improper parental training.

SHORTAGE OF FACILITIES. When facilities (educational, recreational, vocational, etc.) are created, they are done so with the view toward serving a well-defined population. In other words, some facilities are established to serve normal groups (the nonhandicapped). Others are set up for the benefit of the disabled—with rather clear-cut diagnostic criteria (the blind, the deaf, the orthopedically handicapped, the trainable mentally retarded, etc.). Relatively few programs are set up specifically for the mildly handicapped—which is probably one reason that many of these children are found in regular classrooms.

REFERENCES

Baker, Harry J., *Introduction to Special Education*. New York, Macmillan, 1959.
Blackman, Leonard S., and Sparks, Howard L., "What Is Special About Special Education Revisited: The Mentally Retarded." *Exceptional Children*, 31: 242–47 (January, 1965).
Blackman, Leonard S., "The Brave New World of Special Education." Teachers College, Columbia University, N.P., n.d.
Bowden, M. G., and Otto, Henry J., *The Education of the Exceptional Child in Casis School*. Austin, University of Texas, 1964.
Bower, Eli M., "A Process for Identifying Disturbed Children." *Children*, 4: 143–47 (July, 1957).
Child, Irvin L., and Bacon, Margaret K., "Cultural Pressures and Achievement Motivation," in Paul H. Hoch and Joseph Zubin, eds., *Psychopathology of Childhood*. New York, Grune & Stratton, 1955.
Connor, Frances P., "The Education of Crippled Children," in William M.

Cruickshank and G. Orville Johnson, eds., *Education of Exceptional Children and Youth*. Englewood Cliffs, N.J., 1958, pp. 429–97.
Cruickshank, William M., "The Development of Education for Exceptional Children," in William M. Cruickshank and G. Orville Johnson, eds., *Education of Exceptional Children and Youth*. Englewood Cliffs, N.J., Prentice-Hall, 1958.
Cruickshank, William M., "The Exceptional Child in the Elementary and Secondary Schools," in William M. Cruickshank and G. Orville Johnson, eds., *Education of Exceptional Children and Youth*. Englewood Cliffs, N.J., Prentice-Hall, 1958.
Dolch, Edward William, *Helping Handicapped Children in School*. Champaign, Ill., Garrard Press, 1948.
Dunn, Lloyd M., *Exceptional Children in the Schools*. New York, Holt, Rinehart & Winston, 1963.
Freedman, Sanford J., Grunebaum, Henry U., and Greenblatt, Milton, "Perceptual and Cognitive Changes in Sensory Deprivation," in Philip Solomon, et al., eds., *Sensory Deprivation: A Symposium Held at Harvard Medical School*. Cambridge, Mass., Harvard University Press, 1961.
Gesell, Arnold L., and Amatruda, Catherine S., *Developmental Diagnosis*. New York, P. B. Hoeber, 1941.
Glick, Selma J., "Vocational, Educational, and Recreational Needs of the Cerebral Palsied Adult," in Samuel A. Kirk and Bluma Weiner, eds., *Behavior Research on Exceptional Children*. Washington, D.C., The Council for Exceptional Children, NEA, 1963.
Gray, Doris, "The Blind Child in the Regular Classroom," in James F. Magary and John R. Eichorn, eds., *The Exceptional Child: A Book of Readings*. New York, Holt, Rinehart & Winston, 1962, pp. 258–66.
Heider, Grace M., "Adjustment Problems of the Deaf Child," in James F. Magary and John R. Eichorn, eds., *The Exceptional Child: A Book of Readings*. New York, Holt, Rinehart & Winston, 1962, pp. 304–311.
Kirk, Samuel S., *Educating Exceptional Children*. Boston, Houghton Mifflin, 1962.
Kirk, Samuel S., "Basic Fact and Principles Underlying Special Education," in *The Education of Exceptional Children*. National Society for the Study of Education, Forty-Ninth Yearbook, Part II. Chicago, University of Chicago Press, 1950.
Long, Nicholas J., and Newman, Ruth A., "The Teacher and His Mental Health," in Nicholas J. Long, William C. Morse, and Ruth G. Newman, eds., *Conflict in the Classroom*. Belmont, Calif., Wadsworth, 1966.
Mase, Darrel J., "Emotionally Insecure and Disturbed Children," in James F. Magary and John R. Eichorn, eds., *The Exceptional Child: A Book of Readings*. New York, Holt, Rinehart & Winston, 1962, pp. 340–45.

Myklebust, Helmer, *Auditory Disorders in Children.* New York, Grune & Stratton, 1954.

Rimmele, Polly Ann, *Step by Step.* La Salle, Ill., United Cerebral Palsy Associations, 1967.

Roach, Robert E., "The Meaning of Severe Deafness in the Life of a Young Child," in James F. Magary and John R. Eichorn, eds., *The Exceptional Child: A Book of Readings.* New York, Holt, Rinehart & Winston, 1962, pp. 294–303.

Siegel, Ernest, *Helping the Brain Injured Child.* New York, New York Association for Brain Injured Children, 1961.

Strauss, Alfred A., and Kephart, Newell C., *Psychopathology and Education of the Brain-Injured Child,* Vol. II. New York, Grune & Stratton, 1955.

Strauss, Alfred A., and Lehtinen, Laura, *Psychopathology and Education of the Brain-Injured Child,* Vol. I. New York, Grune & Stratton, 1947.

Taft, Lawrence T., "Brain-Injury—Its Definition, Diagnosis, Cause and Treatment." New York, New York Association for Brain Injured Children, n.d.

Tenny, John W., and Lennox, Margaret A., "Children with Epilepsy," in James F. Magary and John R. Eichorn, eds., *The Exceptional Child: A Book of Readings.* New York, Holt, Rinehart & Winston, 1962.

Wooden, Harley Z., "What Is Special About Special Education: The Child Who Is Deaf." *Exceptional Children,* 19: 179–82 (February, 1953).

Wright, Beatrice A., *Physical Disability—A Psychological Approach.* New York, Harper & Brothers, 1960.

CHAPTER

2

The Exceptional Child

The term "exceptional children" denotes all instances of significant deviancy: intellectual—including gifted as well as retarded; physical—including various orthopedic handicaps and chronic health problems; sensorial, *i.e.*, the auditory or visually impaired; social; and emotional. However, only the mentally retarded, the brain-injured and the emotionally disturbed—*i.e.*, children suffering *primarily* from learning and/or behavioral disorders—are considered in this book. Such a distinction is somewhat arbitrary, of course, in that children elude—almost defy—our attempts to create definitive, irrevocable, "either-or" categorization models. In a broad sense, *all* handicapping conditions present some degree of emotional disturbance—the arthritic's pain, the diabetic's strict regimen, the cosmetic problems of the cerebral palsied (grimaces, drooling, etc.), the trauma of accident and surgery, the feeling of the sensorially impaired that they are being left out, the fear brought on by the cardiac's chest pains and the asthmatic's shortness of breath, the morbid prognosis of muscular dystrophy and preoccupation with death. Clearly, all these introduce an emotional component. Similarly, the feeling of being different, the limited ability in performing, the unwholesome environment—ranging from hostility to overprotection—create additional psychological problems for the handicapped. Learning problems can also run "across the board." The preoccupation with physical condition, the sheltered (but limited) surroundings, the frequent educational interruptions brought on by illness, hospitalization, convalescence, etc., can all militate against the development of optimal learning abilities.

Nevertheless, we shall consider only the mentally retarded, the brain-injured and the emotionally disturbed, for these reasons: (1) It is felt that these children constitute the most perplexing and challenging group of pupils to the teacher. (2) They need special consideration since they do not often evoke sympathy and understanding from others as readily as do the physically handicapped (Stullken 1950: 280–81; Siegel 1966: 12, 14). (3) The approach illustrated by this group of children—considering the child's assets and liabilities, viewing the specific problems emanating from the disability and implementing the appropriate classroom modification—is applicable to *all* categories of handicapped children enrolled in regular classrooms.

Moreover, these categories of children are significant in terms of prevalence: Cruickshank (1968) states that the incidence for brain-injury in our country may be as high as 7 percent; the slow learner, IQ 75 to 90, ranges in incidence between 50/1000 to 300/1000, *i.e.* 5 to 30 percent, depending upon socioeconomic level of the community (Kirk 1962: 92); Bower (Trapp and Himelstein 1962: 627) believes that the average class has at least three emotionally disturbed children.

The exceptional population herein considered, then, is meant to be illustrative rather than exhaustive. Moreover, even for this population, we can include only a brief, rather than an intensive, discussion of the various aspects of each category of exceptionality. In general, the aim is to give the regular classroom teacher an overview of the significant aspects of three specific types of exceptional children: the mentally retarded, the brain-injured and the emotionally disturbed. These children's problems (social, psychological and medical, as well as educational) will be emphasized.

Of the above designations, the classification terms used most commonly by educators are "custodial," "trainable" and "educable." Moreover, those falling in the IQ range of 75–89 are often designated as "slow learners" (Johnson 1963: 55). The definition of mental retardation as adopted by the American Association on Mental Deficiency, by considering the upper limit of retardation to be an IQ score of approximately 85, in effect, divides the retarded population into four categories: the custodial, the trainable, the educable and the slow learner (*i.e.*, those slow learners in the 75–85 IQ bracket).

CHARACTERISTICS. Gardner and Nisonger (1962: 122–23, 125) point out some of the distinctive characteristics of the educables and trainables:

> *Educable:* (1) shows a rate of intellectual development which is approximately one-half to three-fourths of that expected of a normal child of the same chronological age . . . ; (2) can be expected to acquire 4th or 5th grade achievement in basic academic subject matter; (3) does not begin formal reading or formal arithmetic skills until between CA 9–12 (MA 6–8); (4) can develop adequate communication skills for ordinary situations; (5) in most instances can develop social and interpersonal adequacy; (6) in most instances can develop occupational skills (skilled and unskilled work) which will result in economic independence in adulthood.
> *Trainable:* (1) shows a mental level and rate of development which is one-fourth to one-half that of the average child; (2) little meaningful knowledge of academic subject matter can be acquired; (3) the mental retardation is frequently accompanied by other physical, sensory-motor and neurological handicaps; (4) social and interpersonal skills of sharing, cooperation, respect for rights of others, etc., can be developed to the extent that retardate can adjust to family and community relations; (5) self-care skills . . . can be developed to the extent that retardate is relatively independent of parent in these areas; (6) work habits and attitudes can be developed to the extent that the retardate can make a limited contribution to his economic support through

engaging in routine household tasks or in simple tasks for remuneration in a supervised setting.*

Goldstein and Seigle (1961) point out that the educable mentally retarded often develop secondary characteristics of frustration-proneness and self-devaluation in addition to their primary intellectual disabilities of oversimplification of concepts (*e.g.,* a tendency to define or describe an object only in terms of its utility—"an orange is for eating"), limited ability to generalize, short memory and attention span, limitations in incidental learning and retarded language development. They do not learn as rapidly, nor do they achieve as much academically as normal children (Peter 1965: 112); moreover, what is learned is not readily transferred to other situations (Blatt 1960).

In general, the educable mentally retarded have similar appearance to normal children, but, as a group, have more physical defects. This is undoubtedly related to causal factors (hereditary as well as environmental) of mental retardation. Johnson (1963: 30–31) states that even the slow learners, as a group, are somewhat smaller and more poorly coordinated than the average population, but that they may be strongly motivated toward sports to compensate for their poor academic performances.

Kough and De Haan (1955: 70) list the following identifying characteristics of slow learners:**

1. Is unable to think abstractly or to handle symbolic materials.
2. Is unable to understand and carry through your directions for assignments.
3. Lacks the so-called "common sense" and reasoning level of the group.

* Reprinted with permission from the January 1962 Monograph Supplement to the *American Journal of Mental Deficiency, 66:* 122–25 *passim.*
** From *Identifying Children with Special Needs* by Jack Kough and Robert De Haan. Science Research Associates, Inc. Reprinted by permission of the publisher.

4. Is unable to understand complex rules of games.
5. Is slow in all areas: academic, social, emotional and physical.
6. Breaks rules of conduct or of games and is often unaware of it.
7. Is unable to work independently.
8. Is easily confused.
9. Has a short interest and attention span.
10. Is unable voluntarily to concentrate.
11. Finds it extremely difficult, if not impossible, to keep up with the class in academic work.
12. Is behind normal grade achievement in school.

Retarded children are often regarded as inferior by their normal counterparts (Baldwin 1958; Siegel 1966). In addition, behavioral problems, even delinquency, can result because of frustrations stemming from discrepancies between the retardate's ability and environmental demands (Blatt 1960).

In short, although the essence of mental retardation is an intellectual deficit, the problem is often compounded by physical lacks as well as by social and emotional maladjustment. Hence, the classroom teacher, in endeavoring to help the slow learner, is by the very nature of the problem, committed to the philosophy of the "whole child."

The Brain-Injured Child

DEFINITION. There is a semantic problem in defining brain injury (Siegel 1961: 13). On the one hand, "brain injury" is a generic term, referring to *any* manifestation of damage to the brain, encompassing such conditions as epilepsy, cerebral palsy, mental retardation and aphasia. There is another variety of brain injury, however, evidenced in perceptual, conceptual and/or behavioral disorders. This variety of brain damage is often referred to simply as "brain-injured." Hence the confusion. "Brain injury" by one definition—the general one—refers to any lesion of the brain. The second definition—the specific one—denotes particular concomitant manifestations—perceptual, conceptual and/or behavioral disorders. This condition, often termed "minimal brain injury," has been defined by Strauss and Lehtinen (1947: 4):

> The brain-injured child is a child who before, during, or after birth has received an injury to or suffered an infection of the brain. As a result of such organic impairment, defects of the neuromotor system may be present or absent; however, such a child may show disturbances in perception, thinking, and emotional behavior, either separately, or in combination.

The overall physiological property of minimal brain injury is thought to be one of imbalance between the old and the new brain (Siegel 1966: 9; Strauss and Lehtinen 1947: 23; Laufer, Denhoff and Solomons 1957: 45–46). This disorganization between the old brain and new brain is believed to cause a faulty "checking mechanism"—*i.e.*, inability to check emotional impulses (Strauss and Lehtinen 1947), as well as a faulty "filtering mechanism"—*i.e.*, inability to refrain from attending to unimportant sensory stimuli (Laufer, Denhoff, and Solomons 1957: 45–46).

Furthermore, this injury is thought to be diffuse as opposed to localized (Doll n.d.: 3; Beck 1961: 59), resulting in disruption in the balanced functioning between old and new brain. This disruption brings about a *general* disordered behavior pattern rather than a specific physical concomitant, which might result from injury to a sharply defined brain territory; however, even when such localized injury occurs, disordered behavior (usually associated with diffuse brain injury) follows (Strauss and Lehtinen 1947: 20, 23).

CHARACTERISTICS. Siegel (1961: 18–23) describes some behavior characteristics which are often assigned to the brain-injured child:*

---

* Reprinted with permission from *Helping the Brain Injured Child* (New York Association for Brain Injured Children, 1961).

1. *Distractibility:* This is, perhaps, his greatest weakness. He is constantly exploring his environment—looking, listening and touching. That which should remain in the background often leaps to the foreground. He is said to be at the mercy of all stimuli. When eating, he will fidget with the silverware. When washing, he may begin an elaborate game with the soap. He gets sidetracked very easily.

He does not always grasp the "wholeness" of what he sees and hears, but perceives only the parts. He may concentrate too much on one isolated letter instead of the word, or on an isolated sound instead of the entire sentence, or the metal tip of the shoelace instead of the complete act of lacing shoes. He may seem inattentive, but actually he is paying attention too well—to background instead of foreground—to parts instead of to "wholes."

2. *Hyperactivity:* The brain-injured child is often overly active. It may be that his hyperactivity is an exaggerated response to stimuli. Not only is he unable to "filter" out the unimportant details of that which he sees, hears, and feels, but he seems unable to control the degree of his reaction. He sees a child—he must touch him. He hears a sound—he must run to investigate its source.

This child, having difficulty in perceiving his environment, does not always react to appropriate stimuli, either mentally, or overtly; therefore, at any given moment, he probably has a surplus of energy. When he *does* react, he does so in an excitable, hyperactive fashion.

3. *Impulsiveness:* In man's development, phylogenetically (from animal to human) as well as ontogenetically (from infant to adult), the direction is always from purely emotional functioning towards reasoned and controlled behavior. Animals snarl and growl when they are angry; babies cry when in pain and scream when frightened. As we mature, our brains develop a "controlling" mechanism, enabling us to inhibit our impulses.

We do not react emotionally to all stimuli. We control any urges we might have to run, scream, cry or laugh loudly. We do not go around indiscriminately touching things and people. We may be talking to someone when, suddenly, we think of something completely extraneous. We generally check the thought and do not interject inappropriate conversation.

The brain-injured child is often unable to control his impulses, and he frequently reacts emotionally. At times, he will say things which do not seem appropriate. This probably happens because he finds difficulty distinguishing between background (his intruding thoughts) and foreground (the conversation at hand), and because he is unable to control the intrusion of his thoughts.

4. *Perseveration:* This child is besieged with all kinds of stimuli, but does not readily integrate them into meaningful, "whole" patterns. When he finally does structure a situation, he seems reluctant to let it go and begin a new one. He finds it difficult to shift from one situation to another. He therefore *perseverates*—continues to respond when the stimulus for such response is no longer there.

A classic example of perseveration is when one continues to pound a nail, even after it has gone all the way into the wood. Such action is not bizarre. It was once appropriate; its inappropriateness lies in its continuous repetition.

Perseveration often occurs after a successful performance. (How much is two and two? Four. How much is three and two? Four. How much is ten and five? Four.) Perhaps this is an effort to recapture the feeling of success, which comes infrequently to these children.

Perseveration is not a predictable factor. It can occur in a variety of situations and in different forms. In writing a word, the brain-injured child may suddenly write one letter over and over again. In crayoning, he often covers an entire page with one color. He may talk about one subject incessantly for months at a time.

One brain-injured child developed an interest in baseball. In addition to constantly chattering about it, and constructing literally hundreds of box scores, he "saw" baseball in instances which were actually unrelated to the game. When his family car, in which he was riding, stopped at a red light, he shouted, "Safe at third!" When he went to the bathroom to urinate, he exclaimed, "Watch the curve ball!"

5. *Irritability:* The brain-injured child is easily irritated. It may be that the task of paying attention to a given situation is

too demanding of him. It may be a manifestation of his inability to interpret reliably the various data of his environment. It may be an expression of his own feelings of inadequacy. It may be a subterfuge, resulting from an unwillingness to react when scolded or reprimanded, followed by a seizing of the next occurrence, however unrelated, to register irritability.

At any rate, a seemingly simple task or a relatively unimportant situation, which to most children might prove only moderately frustrating, can at times produce in the brain-injured child a "catastrophic reaction"—rage, despair, depression, excessive crying, tantrums, withdrawal.

6. *Talkativeness:* The brain-injured child often finds it difficult to perform visuo-motor tasks, activities which require coordination between that which he sees and that which he feels. (He sees the button and the button hole, but may experience considerable difficulty in the actual task of buttoning.)

Because he is unable to do many things, he often resorts to a substitute—talking. He is impulsive, and will talk at the wrong times; he is perseverative, and will say the same thing over and over again.

7. *Awkwardness:* This child is a poor judge of size, shape, distance, direction and relative motion. He may, therefore, trip, fall, and bump into things.

He is not quite sure of his own body in respect to space, and cannot always interpret the messages which the outside world sends to him via his body. He may not sit squarely in his seat, because he cannot "feel" when he is sitting squarely. Running, walking, skipping, even standing still involves this ability of interpreting sensory impressions (the "feel" of the sidewalk against our foot, the sensation of our muscles expanding or contracting, the awareness of our vertical position). The brain-injured child, unable to structure his sensory impressions, often performs poorly in skipping, running, jumping, and hopping.

Then, too, there is the frequent overlap of the various manifestations of brain-injury. The perceptually handicapped child may have additional areas of damage. He may actually present some of the motor impairment of the cerebral palsied. This, obviously, would contribute to his clumsiness.

8. *Poor Speech:* If a child is born completely deaf, it will be

extremely difficult for him to learn to speak. He does not hear others, nor himself, and so has no point of reference.

Hearing, however, implies much more than our ability to receive auditory signals. We must be able to perceive these sounds in sequence, and to assimilate them into meaningful language. We must be able to associate these sounds with our past learnings and experiences.

The brain-injured child may have adequate peripheral hearing, but can suffer from auditory imperception. The word "hospital" may be perceived as "hos-*tip*-al." He may be unable to discriminate between "sh" and "ch" sounds. Instead of hearing "chicken" he may hear (and say) "shicken." He may not see the difference between "put" and "pit."

And again because of overlap in areas of brain damage, the child may actually have impaired hearing, which, of course, would contribute to his poor speech. He may also have motor impairment affecting his organs of speech. This, of course, could be a direct cause of his speech defects.

9. *Destructiveness:* This child is often careless with his belongings; toys, books, pencils, clothing, and other such items are damaged more frequently and with greater rapidity than one would expect (or desire). There is probably a direct relationship between his destructiveness and his perceptual impairment.

If he does not "see" and "feel" things correctly, he is apt to mishandle them. Because he is attracted by all stimuli, he is prone to touch more objects, to explore them too fully, and in so doing, to cause them to break.

Even his perseveration contributes to his destructiveness. If he explores, manipulates, or plays with the same parts of objects over and over again, there is a likelihood that these objects will become damaged.

His destructiveness may also be motivated emotionally. Perhaps he realizes that he is constantly being distracted; he cannot control his attention, and so in frustration, he destroys whatever distracts him—a toy, an article of clothing, or some other belonging.

10. *Animism:* Another peculiar trait of the brain-injured child is that he may be given to animism; that is, he may invest

inanimate objects with life. Hence, two pencils will have a race or two books will fight with each other.

11. *Guilelessness:* This child is often all-trusting and gullible. There is a tendency on his part to accept occurrences without question. He seems to believe the boasts and brags of neighborhood children. These children may make him the "goat" of the crowd, but he doesn't seem to mind. He probably believes in Santa Claus much longer than the average child his age. You can, as the saying goes, sell him the Brooklyn Bridge!

There are several possible explanations for this guilelessness. It may be that his inability to deal in "wholes" and to grasp the essence of his environment causes him to misjudge social situations—to "miss the point."

Or it may be a subterfuge. Perhaps consciously or unconsciously, the brain-injured child has weighed the pro's and con's and decided to accept his role. He may know that the neighborhood children are bragging and boasting, but at least they are talking to him. They are laughing at him, but at least they are not ignoring him. Any contact is better than none.

There is an interesting tangent to this characteristic of guilelessness. Many people (including professionals) who come in contact with brain-injured children, often remark that many of these children are very good-looking youngsters. Perhaps there is something appealing about a child who looks at you wide-eyed, searchingly, lovingly, and without pretense.

12. *Aggressiveness:* These children are often shunned by their peers. Some of them may attempt to "push" their way into the group. In their effort to become accepted—in their search for attention—they may develop aggressive behavior. This aggressiveness, however, does not usually signify hostile intent.

Their impulsiveness and their tendency to reach out and touch people, simply because they are there, also contribute to their aggressiveness.

13. *Social Immaturity:* We would hardly expect a hyperactive, distractible, impulsive, perseverative child, one who is easily irritated, one who performs awkwardly in many areas, to be accepted by his peers. Because he is often excluded from the group, he necessarily is lacking in social experiences. This makes

him even more socially immature. He often relates better with younger children.

His social immaturity, then, is not necessarily a trait in itself; more likely, it is a reflection of all the perceptual, conceptual and behavioral disorders existent in this child.

Krupp and Schwartzberg (1960: 65) list four broad areas of defect which are generally ascribed to brain-injured children:

(1) Faulty powers of inhibition and control, motor and emotional; the child is forced into actions that are not intended. (2) Disturbances of perception. Perception is more than receiving stimuli; it is an act or a process in which meanings are attributed to the sensed stimuli. (3) Predisposition to anxiety due to impaired organization, confused interpretation of the environment, and early postural reflex disturbance. The child has impaired visual-motor performance, with a corresponding inability to distinguish foreground figures and background details. There is a sort of confusing-the-forest-for-the-trees response. Distortions of body image are also present. (4) Secondary psychological defense mechanisms related to the repeated frustrations (anxiety) encountered by the brain-injured child and his parents. These may be character reactions such as meticulousness, clinging or withdrawal; psychoneurotic reactions such as phobias, obsessions, and compulsions; psychotic reactions such as schizophrenic thinking disturbances and specific disabilities.*

These traits, of course, describe brain-injured children as a group: It would be wrong to ascribe automatically the entire syndrome to each brain-injured child. Not *all* of the brain-injured exhibit *all* of these traits. Their major characteristics seem to be hyperactivity, distractibility, impulsiveness, perseveration and irritability—yet even this must be regarded as a generalization. Some brain-injured children exhibit all of these characteristics, others only a few.

* Reprinted with permission from the February 1960 issue *Social Casework,* *41:* 65, published by the Family Service Association of America.

It should be remembered, also, that there are varying degrees of behavior disorder. One child may be extremely distractible and hyperactive, another might be only mildly so. The hyperactivity and distractibility, in each case, may be the clue pointing to brain injury.

Nevertheless, because these symptoms so often appear, we are on fairly safe ground when we say that brain-injured children *generally* are hyperactive, distractible, impulsive, perseverative and irritable.

It is when we consider some of the other possible manifestations that we see the necessity for avoiding positive, dogmatic statements. Indeed, we cannot even generalize.

For example, it would be incorrect to state that brain-injured children are generally aggressive. The most one should say here is that some are and some aren't. As a matter of fact, there are some brain-injured children who are quite the opposite of aggressive. Because they function at an immature social level, and because perceptual impairment limits their ability at self-defense, these children are often picked on and ridiculed. They will not harm others; they themselves are the ones who get hurt.

Another factor which makes it difficult to assess the total nature of the brain-injured child is the "scatter" in his level of achievement. The quality of his functioning in various areas is not uniform but varies from activity to activity, and is often widespread and scattered. He may verbalize extremely well, yet perform poorly. He may be a good reader, but probably does not write as well. He may exhibit a more than adequate memory, yet may be unable to assimilate and utilize the facts that he remembers. He probably does not make the most of his strengths.

This "scatter" further contributes to the erratic quality of his functioning. Moreover, it underlines the necessity of viewing each brain-injured child as first and foremost an individual.

Many brain-injured children have both learning and behavior problems; others possess problems of only one type. Brain injury frequently overlaps with other diagnoses, so that the same brain-injured child may also be mentally retarded; however, it is quite possible for a brain-injured child to present learning problems emanating not from mental retardation, but from basic perceptual impairment.

There are many brain-injured children who are placed in regular classes—indeed, some can be found even in classes for the gifted. Very often, their "behavioral" problems consist of disorganization, poor self-concept, social immaturity and general anxiety—traits that make them problems to themselves rather than to others.

Many writers (Doll n.d.: 3–6; Krupp and Schwartzberg 1960: 66; Laufer, Denhoff and Solomons 1957; Thelander, Phelps and Kirk 1958: 409) have stated that the prognosis for the minimally brain-injured child is favorable, provided that he is not significantly handicapped by cerebral palsy or mental retardation, and provided that he receives appropriate education and management. It is of utmost importance that he receive acceptance and psychological support from those with whom he comes in contact, thus reducing anxiety while simultaneously bolstering positive self-concept.

The Emotionally Disturbed Child

SEMANTIC PROBLEM. The term "emotionally disturbed" also presents a problem in semantics. On the one hand (as with the term "brain-injured"), there is a generic connotation: *i.e.,* to many professionals as well as laymen, *all* behavioral problems— covert as well as overt, mild or severe, the aggressive or the withdrawn child, the "sick" as well as the "bad"—are subsumed under this term. In *Teaching the Emotionally Disturbed: A Casebook,* for example, Grossman (1965) includes the disruptive and the aggressive child as well as the neurotic and the schizophrenic. Similarly, in *Conflict in the Classroom: The Edu-*

cation of Emotionally Disturbed Children, Long, Morse and Newman (1966) describe the maladjusted, the delinquent and the culturally deprived "latchkey" children (so-called because both parents work, necessitating their entry, by latchkey, into their empty homes), as well as the schizophrenic. In short, under this broad connotation of the term "emotionally disturbed" are subsumed psychotics, neurotics, those with character disorders, the socially maladjusted, the delinquent, drug addicts, and others.

There is, however, a narrower meaning to this term. Many authors do not regard "emotionally disturbed" as encompassing the gamut of subcategories. To them, a psychotic would be considered emotionally *ill* rather than merely *disturbed*. Specifically, in the limited rather than the umbrella version, the term "emotionally disturbed" tends to be more or less synonymous with the term "neurotic." This has not really been spelled out in the literature but has evolved through usage and mutual acceptance. Occasionally, though, one finds evidence of this in print. For example, when Heber (1959: 40) presented his classification system of mental retardates, one category he defined was "psychogenic mental retardation associated with emotional disturbance." This included "cases of mental retardation associated with a history of a prolonged *emotional disturbance (neurotic disorder)* dating from an early age [italics added]. . . ."

In summary, then, the semantic problem raised by the term "emotionally disturbed" is that there are two connotations: The generic concept would include all possible atypical behavior, *including* the neurotic; whereas the specific designation is the neurotic only.

CLASSIFICATION AND DEFINITION. There have been attempts by educators to classify the various atypical behavior patterns into a meaningful system so that those working with the children involved might more fully grasp the nature and needs of their problems. A logical beginning has been to separate the "sick" from the "bad." Pate (1963: 240) points out that for purposes of planning educational programs, these children are divided into two categories: (1) "the emotionally disturbed children suffer from mental illness" and (2) "socially maladjusted children are chronic juvenile offenders who regularly disregard broader social values and rules as a matter of course, substituting in their stead the values and rules of their peer group." Kirk (1962: 330–31) uses the term "behavior deviation" as the generic term encompassing "that behavior of a child which (1) has a detrimental effect on his development and adjustment and/or (2) interferes with the lives of other people." Under this term, however, he makes two classifications: The *emotionally disturbed children* are those "who have inner tensions and show anxiety, neuroticism or psychotic behavior" whereas the *socially maladjusted* are those children whose behavior is outside the range of the "culturally permissible" in that they have repeated conflicts with and interfere with the lives of others (family, classmates and teachers, community).

It should be pointed out that there are other factors in the classification of the emotionally disturbed. To begin with, many of the subgroups can, in turn, be further subdivided. For example, the term "psychotic" applies to the schizophrenic, the manic-depressive, the paranoid, possibly the autistic, and others. Similarly, the term "neurotic" includes anxiety states, neurasthenia, reactive neurosis, compulsion, hysteria, traumatic neurosis, etc. (Landis and Bolles 1947). There can be further classification based on medical concepts, on personality traits (*e.g.,* schizoid, cycloid, introversion-extroversion, etc.) or even on physical constitution or body build—the so-called Kretschmer classification of asthenic, athletic, pyknic and dysplastic, and later extending to Sheldon's endomorph, mesomorph and ectomorph (Hall and Lindsay 1957: 336–75).

Despite the variety of possible classification systems, the one that seems most useful for educational purposes (*i.e.,* screening, placement, curriculum development, methods, etc.) seems to be the rather oversimplified dichotomous division of the emotionally disturbed (*i.e.,* the ill) and the socially maladjusted.

In defining the emotionally disturbed children, Haring (1963: 291) states that they chronically evidence (1) inability to learn which cannot be explained on the basis of intellectual, sensory-motor or physical deficits, (2) inability to develop interpersonal relationships, (3) inappropriate responses to day-to-day life situations, and (4) a variety of excessive behavior displays, ranging from impulsivity to withdrawal. Authorities (Blackham 1967: 73–74; Morse 1958: 158) agree that the intensity, frequency and duration of the questionable behavior under consideration are valid criteria of emotional disturbance. Blackham (1967: 75–76) lists inadequate self-concept as a major cause of maladaptive behavior (*e.g.,* insatiable need for continuous reassurances, magnifying a relatively minor flaw, inability to accept genuine praise graciously, a steadfast avoidance of competitive situations, a refusal to do schoolwork, overall depression, unconscious acts of self-punishment and self-destruction, even the entertainment of suicidal thoughts).

The socially maladjusted include the truant, delinquent, incorrigible, behavior-problem cases. Kirk (1962: 331) states that "they are unmanageable in the home . . . generally problems in school, retarded in educational achievements, destructive, quarrelsome, and often socially immature. . . ."

In any categorizing model, we conscientiously seek similarities, while de-emphasizing individual differences, hence losing some information (Siegel 1968: 433). Therefore *any* classification system will possess some limitations. Nosologic and definitional models in the behavioral sciences seem particularly vulnerable to error—or at least confusion. This is so for many reasons: (1) The child is a growing—and changing—organism, and therefore it is difficult to pinpoint a given moment or action as being a statistically reliable sample of his totality. (2) We can only measure and observe symbols, symptoms and effects, rather than the condition itself—*i.e.*, we can observe and quantify IQ test results and *imply* that we are measuring intelligence. Sometimes we can observe a behavioral display and *surmise* that we are witnessing an emotional disturbance. (3) Normal children at times may perform abnormal acts, and conversely most disturbed children often demonstrate some periods of normal functioning and adequate control (Morse 1958: 158). Such guidelines as *"general* mode of behavior" or "consistency" or "effectiveness," while perhaps of some help in creating a line of demarcation between the normal and the abnormal subject, are far from being infallible diagnostic instruments. (4) Overlapping contributes to the complexity of the picture. Simplicity would demand that children fall clearly under one nomenclatural title or another, but the fact remains that the same child may have several handicaps—*e.g.*, many brain-injured children are also emotionally disturbed; some emotionally disturbed individuals are mentally retarded; some culturally deprived are socially maladjusted, etc. Even within the sole category of behavioral deviancy, subcategories often overlap: The child who is emotionally disturbed (*i.e.*, "sick") may exhibit socially maladjusted behavior in his conduct toward others; if this behavior is in conflict with the law, the child may then be adjudged delinquent—delinquency being a subgroup under the socially maladjusted (Kirk 1962: 331–32). (5) There is a commonality of symptoms which cuts across different areas of exceptionality. Brain-injured children generally demonstrate perceptual problems—but so do many emotionally disturbed children. Severely emotionally disturbed children have difficulties in abstract thinking—but so do the mentally retarded. All three groups are often anxious, socially immature and have low self-esteem. It is equally true that the autistic, the schizophrenic, the aphasic and the peripherally deaf are among those children evidencing language disorders. (6) Making the diagnostic boundary lines still more hazy is the factor of intragroup variability. That is, within the given group of the emotionally disturbed, one finds considerable variability between one subject and another. One child may have a learning problem while another does not. One may demonstrate incoordination while another possesses considerable athletic and mechanical aptitude. Different emotionally disturbed children have dissimilar coping mechanisms, unique personalities, individual preferences, varied sources of motivation and different backgrounds. (7) An extension of intragroup variability is the existence of subgroups within a subgroup. For example, the socially maladjusted—a subgroup of the generic category of emotional disturbance—can itself be splintered. Hewitt and Jenkins (1946) studied three varieties of the socially maladjusted—the unsocialized aggressive, the socialized aggressive and the overinhibited. (8) Also to be taken into account is the subjectivity of the diagnostician. Clearly, one diagnostician may consider a given act normal while another may regard it as pathological. Culture and ecology (Rhodes 1967: 449–50) are similar determinants. For example, physical assault may be interpreted as a crime, a sickness or perhaps a sin depending upon which cultural institution does the labeling.

CHARACTERISTICS.

1. *Emotionally disturbed.* Much has been written concerning the characteristics of emotionally disturbed persons (texts in abnormal psychology, clinical research, vignettes and case histories, etc.). Several basic clinical syndromes exist that can be of interest to the classroom teacher:

Psychotics have difficulty dealing with reality (*i.e.*, in differentiating fact from fantasy). Hallucinations, delusions and bizarre language are frequently present. They often "screen out" people. *Childhood schizophrenia* is an important variety of psychosis—in terms of both its prevalence and of the concern of professionals with it. Another variety of psychosis is *childhood autism* (Kanner and Eisenberg 1955: 228, 232–33), characterized by (a) extreme withdrawal tendencies—*i.e.*, a desire to be alone, and (b) a resistance to change. In addition, autistic children have severe communication problems, ranging from no speech at all to speech marked with pronoun confusion.

The *neurotic* has no loss of contact with reality. He has good insight into—but no control of—his problems. He is not a danger to himself or to others (as is the psychotic), but he may be a nuisance. He can be further characterized by tension, depression, anxiety, guilt feelings, phobias and a preoccupation with personal problems (Landis and Bolles 1947: 531–33).

Psychopathic personalities often perform antisocial acts but are not troubled by guilt feelings. They show no positive response to kindness, a disregard for truth, tenuous emotional ties (*i.e.*, no capacity for love), rebellion against authority, superficial attractiveness but overall unreliability, and no anxiety (Krippner 1963). They are sometimes referred to as *sociopathic personalities* or *character disorders*.

The *school phobic* is the child who is petrified and overwhelmed by school. It is a severe reaction and is to be distinguished from the "'natural aversion" to school which many normal children profess. Upon investigation, it turns out that the mother's extreme anxiety over the separation is somehow transmitted to the child, manifesting itself in a fear of school (Eisenberg 1962).

Psychosomatic disorders are emotional disturbances resulting in actual physical malfunctioning. Some common examples are ulcers, severe eczema, headaches, even asthma. Although these illnesses may have an emotional basis, they are as real as though their etiology had been purely physical, and are therefore to be distinguished from the "ailments" of malingerers, who feign physical illness.

Some guides (*i.e., general* characteristics), as opposed to specific clinical syndromes, have been set up (Kough and De Haan 1955: 62), which may enable the classroom teacher to assist in the identification of the emotionally disturbed. These authors point out that such a child:

1. Needs an unusual amount of prodding to get work completed.
2. Is inattentive and indifferent, or apparently lazy.
3. Exhibits nervous mannerisms such as nail biting, sucking thumb or fingers, stuttering, extreme restlessness, muscle twitching, hair twisting, picking and scratching, deep and frequent sighing.
4. Is actively excluded by most of the children whenever they get the chance.
5. Is a failure in school for no apparent cause.
6. Is absent from school frequently or dislikes school intensely.
7. Seems to be more unhappy than most of the children.
8. Achieves much less in school than his ability indicates he should.
9. Is jealous or overcompetitive.*

2. *Socially maladjusted.* The basic characteristic of the socially maladjusted child is his social maladjustment—a definition within a definition! For example, it has been pointed out (Hewitt and Jenkins 1946) that: (a) the *unsocialized aggressive* behavior syndrome consists of assaultive tendencies, cruelty, open defiance toward authority (but in isolation rather than in gang activities), malicious mischief and paucity of guilt feelings; (b) the *socialized delinquent* is characterized by association with undesirable companions, gang activities, defiance of authority but demonstration of peer loyalty, truancy and running away from home; and (c) the *overinhibited* behavior syndrome consists of shyness, timidity, withdrawal and seclusion, apathy, worrying, sensitivity and submissiveness.

Delinquents, as a group, have characteristics which separate them from nondelinquents. Clearly, the delinquent act is the outstanding difference. However, other identifying traits have also been found (Glueck and Glueck 1950: 281–82): (a) a solid, muscular, closely knit physical build—the so-called meso-

* From *Identifying Children with Special Needs* by Jack Kough and Robert De Haan. Science Research Associates, Inc. Reprinted by permission of the publisher.

morphic type; (b) energetic but restless, impulsive, aggressive, destructive, extroverted and (c) a direct and concrete mode of problem solving and communication as opposed to a more symbolic or intellectual style.

ETIOLOGY. The causes of emotional disturbance seem to lie somewhere between heredity and environment. As Landis and Bolles (1946: 81) state, "The general consensus seems to be that there is a constitutional predisposition (a genetically determined lack of resistance) to neurotic behavior, so that the amount of stress necessary to bring out such reactions varies among individuals. . . . If there are relatively few stresses in the environment, a person may not show obvious neurotic tendencies, even though a constitutional inadequacy is present. . . ." Thus, a neurotic style of life—characterized by preoccupation with personal problems, feelings of self-reproach and inadequacy, inability to "get along" in everyday situations and a prevailing anxious and unhappy mood—is born of two factors: (1) a psychologically inadequate constitution and (2) exposure to psychosocial factors conducive to insecurity during early childhood (Landis and Bolles 1946: 81).

The inappropriate coping mechanisms can be viewed as both causes and effects of emotional disturbance. Grossman (1965: 9-13, 16-18) delineates three modes of interpersonal relationship, *i.e.*, the maneuvers that the emotionally disturbed utilize in their endeavor to bring about a desired reaction from others:

(1) *Moving against others*. These children are disruptive and aggressive, attacking, accusing and blaming others.

(2) *Moving toward others*. These children are rigidly conforming. They are friendly and cooperative, primarily because of feelings of inadequacies, and fear that others may attack them if they are not ingratiating.

(3) *Moving away from others*. These children are given to daydreaming and are reluctant to participate in interpersonal relationships. They are withdrawn, they do not volunteer and they shy away from situations in which they must discuss them-

selves or their personal opinions. They may speak in faint, almost inaudible, tones.

Research shows the effect of severe emotional deprivation in early childhood upon behavior. Goldfarb (1944) demonstrated that children who were institutionalized during early childhood (4 to 5 months to 4 years of age) were impaired in areas of control, perception and goal-directed behavior when compared to children who were placed in foster homes. (It is important to note that although the study occurred when the subjects were between ages 10 and 14 years, the effects of the earlier institutionalization were still significant.)

Kanner and Eisenberg (1955: 228–29) found that autistic children generally had "sophisticated" parents (*i.e.*, one or both were college graduates), "refrigerator"-type mothers, and fathers who rarely played with their children. There was an implied relationship between the personalities, attitudes and child-rearing practices of the parents and the pathology of the child.

Socioeconomic and psychosocial factors are correlated with social maladjustment. Hewitt and Jenkins (1946) found idiosyncratic clusters of background traits surrounding each of the three delineated categories of socially maladjusted children: (1) The unsocialized, aggressive children came from broken homes; many were illegitimate and were unwanted by their mothers in infancy. (2) The socialized aggressive came from broken homes, but they had positive relations with their mothers in early infancy. They were later rejected; however, it is implied that the security which they received in early childhood was sufficient to enable them to form some kind of interpersonal ties—albeit, with gang members. (3) The overinhibited children came from families of higher economic means. They were frequently rejected by their parents—this rejection assuming the form of overprotection.

Glueck and Glueck (1950) contrasted 500 delinquents with a control group of 500 nondelinquents, matching both groups in age, IQ, ethnic background and residence in underprivileged neighborhoods. It was found that the delinquents' families moved more frequently, had more crowded and less sanitary homes and were more often recipients of welfare aid. Both the paternal and maternal families of the delinquents had more instances of mental retardation, emotional disturbance, alcoholism and criminality. There was a greater proportion of forced marriages among the delinquents' parents. There was less adult supervision. Discipline was harsh and inconsistent.

Robison (1964: 116) points out that whether or not the factors of poverty, broken homes or working mothers actually cause delinquency, certainly the *meaning* that these situations hold for the child is paramount.

A major tenet regarding the cause of behavioral deviations is the "concept of discrepancy" (Kirk 1962: 336) : There is a gap between the child's capacity to behave and the requirements of the environment; this discrepancy results in frustration, which, in turn, results in behavior problems. Kirk (1962: 338) states that this tenet does not explain the etiology of all behavioral deviations and that the psychosocial factors of (1) early home experiences and (2) social and economic conditions of the child's environment are equally important determinants of behavior.

The classroom teacher has a vital role in the prevention—or, certainly, in the amelioration—of emotional disturbance in children. Logically, the school could be the focal point of positive psychological forces for the disturbed (or the potentially disturbed—and this includes the brain-injured and mentally retarded child, as well). Here, self-concepts can be strengthened, anxieties reduced, peer approval nourished. The child who finds emotional insecurity in the home or in the street desperately needs to encounter security and acceptance in school. The child with negative social values, inappropriate behavioral modes and paucity of motivation, must be gently, (and often, subtly) led—not shoved—into proper guidelines. He needs sup-

The Exceptional Child

port, not rejection; warmth, not intolerance; hope, not despair.

Ironically, the school, instead of saving the troubled child, all too often becomes the psychological straw that breaks the camel's back (Conrad 1951: 30–32, 86, 94–95). The wrong is compounded in that emotional disturbance can often be corrected—that is, *cured*—via a good mental hygiene approach. The classroom teacher cannot cure mental retardation or deafness or brain-injury or cerebral palsy, but in the case of emotional disturbance, the teacher's know-how and attitude may enable him to reverse the original diagnosis.

The topic of mental illness has always fascinated us. Perhaps this is so because in each of us lies the entire range of mental illness. Long, Morse and Newman (1966: 1) explain:

> Our nightmares, if they serve no other purpose, enable us to share the ways in which many psychotics experience life . . . [our] sudden loss of temper . . . gives [us] a momentary empathy with the feelings of uncontrollable rage, helplessness, confusion, guilt and self-hate felt by the child with no impulse control. Most of us have shared a variety of neurotic symptoms: the terrifying fear of something that we know rationally should not in itself cause fear; the magical, protective cloak of knocking on wood, crossing fingers; the compulsive need to get one thing done, no matter how inane or how inconvenient, before we can do something else; . . . the headaches, stomach pains, or shortness of breath (unexplainable in the doctor's office) that often occur at a family reunion, at exam time, or at the appearance of a certain individual; the need to eat greedily though one is unhungry; . . . the uncontrollable blush or stutter; the immobilizing lapse of memory; the urge to . . . say the very thing that will get us into trouble, or the urge to be silent when speaking up might simplify our lives.*

Perhaps this realization that we, too, at times function in an emotionally disturbed pattern can give us real insight into the

* Reprinted with permission from *Conflict in the Classroom: The Education of Emotionally Disturbed Children* (Belmont, Calif., Wadsworth, 1966).

needs of these children, can suggest ameliorative methodology and can instill in us compassion, thereby replacing negative attitudes such as "he rubs me the wrong way," "if his parents can't do anything with him, how can I" or "show me an emotionally disturbed child, and I'll show you an emotionally disturbed mother."

In this area of psychological support, the needs of the emotionally disturbed child coincide completely with those of all handicapped children—including mentally retarded and the brain-injured. That is to say, children who are handicapped, sensing their "differentness," become sensitive, develop fragile egos, and deplete—often to the point of bankruptcy—their inner reserves and resources. All children need acceptance, but the normal child, having more positive self-concept is better able to cope with defeat. Thus, a good mental hygiene approach on the part of the classroom teacher, one that is supportive and accepting is, for the handicapped child, a curricular priority.

REFERENCES

Baldwin, Willie Kate, "The Educable Mentally Retarded Child in the Regular Grades." *Exceptional Children*, Vol. 25, No. 3 (November, 1958) pp. 106–108, 112.

Beck, Harry S., "Detecting Psychological Symptoms of Brain-Injury." *Exceptional Children*, 28: 57–62 (September, 1961).

Blackham, Garth J., *The Deviant Child in the Classroom*. Belmont, Calif., Wadsworth, 1967.

Blatt, Burton, "Some Persistently Recurring Assumptions Concerning the Mentally Retarded." *Training School Bulletin*, 57: 48–59 (August, 1960).

Bower, Eli M., "Comparison of the Characteristics of Identified Emotionally Disturbed Children with Other Children in Classes," in E. Philip Trapp and Philip Himelstein, eds., *Readings on the Exceptional Child*. New York, Appleton-Century-Crofts, 1962, pp. 610–28.

Conrad, Earl, *The Public School Scandal*. New York, John Day, 1951.

Cruickshank, William M., *The Brain-Injured Child in Home, School, and Community*. Syracuse, N.Y., Syracuse University Press, 1967.

Doll, Edgar A., "The Essentials of an Inclusive Concept of Mental Deficiency." *American Journal on Mental Deficiency*, Vol. 46, No. 2 (October, 1941), pp. 214–219.

Doll, Edgar A., *Behavior Syndromes of CNS Impairment.* A Devereaux Reprint. Devon, Pa., Devereaux Schools, n.d.
Eisenberg, Leon, "School Phobia: A Study in the Communication of Anxiety," in E. Philip Trapp and Philip Himelstein, eds., *Readings on the Exceptional Child.* New York, Appleton-Century-Crofts, 1962, pp. 629–39.
Gardner, William L., and Nisonger, Hershel W., "A Manual on Program Development in Mental Retardation." A Monograph Supplement. *American Journal of Mental Deficiency,* Vol. 66, No. 4 (January, 1962).
Glueck, Sheldon, and Glueck, Eleanor, *Unraveling Juvenile Delinquency.* New York, The Commonwealth Fund, 1950.
Goldfarb, William, "Effects of Early Institutional Care on Adolescent Personality: Rorschach Data." *American Journal of Orthopsychiatry,* 14: 441–47, 1944.
Goldstein, Herbert, and Seigle, Dorothy M., "Characteristics of Educable Mentally Handicapped Children," in Jerome H. Rothstein, ed., *Mental Retardation: Readings and Resources.* New York, Holt, Rinehart & Winston, 1961.
Grossman, Herbert, *Teaching the Emotionally Disturbed: A Casebook.* New York, Holt, Rinehart & Winston, 1965.
Hall, Calvin S., and Lindsay, Gardner, *Theories of Personality.* New York, John Wiley & Sons, 1957.
Haring, Norris G., "The Emotionally Disturbed," in Samuel Kirk and Bluma Weiner, eds., *Behavioral Research on Exceptional Children.* NEA, 1963, pp. 291–317.
Heber, Rick, "A Manual on Terminology and Classification in Mental Retardation." Monograph Supplement to *American Journal of Mental Deficiency,* 64: 3–111 (September, 1959).
Hewitt, Lester Eugene, and Jenkins, Richard L., "Fundamental Patterns of Maladjustment: The Dynamics of Their Origin," Springfield, Ill., Michigan Child Guidance Institute, 1946.
Johnson, G. Orville, *Education for the Slow Learner.* Englewood Cliffs, N.J., Prentice-Hall, 1963.
Kanner, Leo, and Eisenberg, Leon, "Notes on the Follow-up Studies of Autistic Children," in Paul H. Hoch and Joseph Zubin, eds., *Psychopathology of Childhood.* New York, Grune & Stratton, 1955, pp. 227–39.
Kirk, Samuel A., *Educating Exceptional Children.* Boston, Houghton Mifflin, 1962.
Kirk, Samuel A., *Public School Provisions for the Severely Retarded Children:* Special Report to the New York State Interdepartmental Health Resources Board. Albany, N.Y., July, 1957.
Kough, Jack, and De Haan, Robert F., *Identifying Children with Special Needs,* Vol. I. Chicago, Science Research Associates, 1955.

Krippner, Stanley, "Sociopathic Tendencies and Reading Retardation in Children." *Exceptional Children*, 29: 258–66 (February, 1963).

Krupp, George R., and Schwartzberg, Bernard, "The Brain-Injured Child: A Challenge to Social Workers." *Social Casework*, 41: 63–69 (February, 1960).

Landis, Carney, and Bolles, M. Marjorie, *Textbook of Abnormal Psychology*. New York, Macmillan, 1947.

Laufer, Maurice W., Denhoff, Eric, and Solomons, Gerald, "Hyperkinetic Impulse Disorder in Children's Behavior Problems." *Psychosomatic Medicine*, Vol. 19 (January, 1957), pp. 45–46.

Long, Nicholas J., Morse, William C., and Newman, Ruth G., *Conflict in the Classroom: The Education of Emotionally Disturbed Children*. Belmont, Calif., Wadsworth, 1966.

Morse, William C., "The Education of Socially Maladjusted and Emotionally Disturbed Children," in William M. Cruickshank and G. Orville Johnson, eds., *Education of Exceptional Children and Youth*. Englewood Cliffs, N.J., Prentice-Hall, 1958, pp. 557–608.

Pate, John E., "Emotionally Disturbed and Socially Maladjusted Children," in Lloyd M. Dunn, ed., *Exceptional Children in the School*. New York, Holt, Rinehart & Winston, 1963, pp. 239–84.

Peter, Laurence J., *Prescriptive Teaching*. New York, McGraw-Hill, 1965.

Rhodes, William C., "The Disturbing Child: A Problem of Ecological Management." *Exceptional Children*, 33: 7 (March, 1967), pp. 449–55.

Robison, Sophia M., *Juvenile Delinquency: Its Nature and Control*. New York, Holt, Rinehart & Winston, 1964.

Siegel, Ernest, "Learning Disabilities: Substance or Shadow." *Exceptional Children*, Vol. 34, No. 6 (February, 1968), pp. 433–37.

Siegel, Ernest, "Special Education and Human Relations." *The Digest of Mentally Retarded*, Vol. 3, No. 1 (Fall, 1966).

Siegel, Ernest, *A Comparison of Minimally Brain-Injured Children of Normal Intelligence with Non-Handicapped Children in Tactual Discrimination Abilities*, Unpublished Ed. D. Dissertation. New York, Teachers College, Columbia University, 1966.

Siegel, Ernest, *Helping the Brain Injured Child*. New York, New York Association for Brain Injured Children, 1961.

Skeels, Harold M., as quoted in "Environment Important." *Science News*, Vol. 90, No. 1 (October, 1966), p. 248.

Strauss, Alfred A., and Lehtinen, Laura E., *Psychopathology and Education of the Brain-Injured Child*, Vol. I. New York, Grune & Stratton, 1947.

Stullken, Edward H., "Special Schools and Classes for the Socially Maladjusted," in *The Education of Exceptional Children*, National Society for the Study of Education, Forty-ninth Yearbook, Part II. Chicago, University of Chicago Press, 1950.

Thelander, H. E., Phelps, Jane K., and Kirk, E. Walton, "Learning Disabilities Associated with Lesser Brain Damage." *Journal of Pediatrics,* Vol. 53, No. 4 (October, 1958), pp. 405–409.

Tredgold, A. F., *A Textbook of Mental Deficiency.* New York, William Wood & Co., 1937.

Wechsler, David, "The IQ Is an Intelligent Test." *The New York Times Magazine,* June 26, 1966.

CHAPTER

3

The Teacher's Role: Techniques for Solving Nine Basic Problems

Despite the different kinds of children (brain-injured, mentally retarded, emotionally disturbed) being discussed here, there are many areas of commonality insofar as their specific learning and/or behavioral problems are concerned./ Disability in reading, for example, is quite common among these children, related perhaps to the retardate's difficulty with symbol manipulation, the brain-injured child's perceptual impairment and the emotionally disturbed child's "learning blocks." A poor self-concept is probably a basic factor with which *all* handicapped children must cope, and social immaturity is another problem common to these children. \

In many instances, the teacher might profitably make the same kind of modification regardless of the etiology of the problem—*e.g.*, a perceptually impaired child, another child with poor muscular coordination and an emotionally disturbed child who finds it difficult to work for a sustained length of time may each present problems in writing tasks; the same modification—smaller doses—would probably be of some benefit to each. Similarly, a multisensory approach could help a brain-injured child get intersensory "feedback," might tend to concretize the lesson for the retardate and could serve as a motivational source for the apathetic or negative emotionally disturbed child.

Needless to say, the identical "remedy" is not indicated in all cases, and diagnostic nomenclature *is* important. For example, brain-injured children often require the structure of reduced stimuli so as to diminish foreground-background confusion (Strauss and Lehtinen 1947; Cruickshank *et al.* 1961). However, a stimulus-rich environment, where there are varied objects to see, manipulate and experience, can often prove effective in the improvement of intellectual development of the cultural-familial retarded child (Peter 1965: 38), the emotionally disturbed child (Rhodes 1966: 407) and the culturally deprived child (Riessman 1962: 63–73; Fremont 1966: 318).

When practical suggestions are reduced in writing to the essential elements of classroom approaches, techniques and modifications, there is always the danger of creating a finished written product which has an unsophisticated, "cookbook" flavor; however, when one realizes that the suggestions are based on research, formal as well as informal (observation and experience, discussions with professionals, "buzz" sessions in education courses, etc.) a degree of validity emerges.

Then, too, it may be that the search for the new, the sophisticated, the innovative and the dramatic have led educators down blind alleys, and perhaps many of the answers *do* lie in the undramatic and common-sense approaches. For example, what can a regular classroom teacher do to help a child who has poor vision? Some seemingly obvious suggestions are: alternate board work with seat work, keep glasses clean and properly adjusted, eliminate glare, avoid creating shadows by bending over a child while working with him, avoid excessive and unnecessary reading, etc. (Pelone 1962: 271–75). What can be done to help a hard-of-hearing child who is enrolled in a regular classroom? Again, some obvious answers are: allow him to sit where he can hear, teachers and classmates should face the light when talking, and speak clearly and distinctly, etc. (Streng 1962: 293).

The point we wish to make is this: The fact that suggestions may seem obvious, intuitive or undramatic does not diminish their value. In brief, approaches that are "common sense" are not necessarily commonplace.

The educational and/or psychological problems presented in this section were selected on the basis of four criteria: (1) *frequency, i.e.,* only if they tend to occur relatively frequently among the mildly handicapped school population under discussion; (2) *commonality, i.e.,* if they tend to occur among all three categories of exceptional children under discussion; (3) *significance, i.e.,* only serious, weighty, important problems—not trivial ones—were considered; and (4) *feasibility*—problems were considered only when it seemed feasible to include the suggested ameliorative techniques in a regular classroom program.

Poor Self-Concept

It is generally agreed that children who have learning problems and/or those who are behaviorally impaired often develop a poor self-concept (Dunn 1963: 113; Frostig and Horne 1962: 11–12). Their feelings of inadequacy are probably fed from two major streams: (1) inability to perform adequately related to specific perceptual, conceptual or emotional impairment and (2) lack of sympathy, understanding and acceptance of others toward them. The negative self-image, often anxiety provoking, is self-defeating, thereby creating a downward spiral: Difficulty in perceiving and utilizing sensory data leads to inadequate performance (learning as well as behavior), resulting in non-acceptance; anxiety and feelings of inadequacy and self-reproach ensue, resulting in even poorer performance; scorn, rebuffs and hostility accrue in ever-increasing frequency.

The astute classroom teacher may be instrumental in breaking this cycle. Obviously, his own attitude toward the child with problems is paramount. If he, too, rejects him, this serves to corroborate the child's self-doubts and feelings of worthlessness. Then, too, the child's peers generally reflect the teacher's attitude toward him (Graver 1962: 374; Harper and Wright 1962: 366).

In general, a firm but supportive attitude toward the child is recommended—"firm" denoting consistency, structure, expectations; "supportive" implying acceptance and patience as well as sheer know-how.

A good starting point is for the teacher to become acquainted with the child's case history. The mere factor of diagnosis (even the "labeling" connotation of diagnosis) can be of value. After all, the teacher is less likely to regard a child's poor behavior or performance (forgetfulness, disorganization, poor penmanship, sloppiness, impulsivity, etc.) as pure willfulness when the medical/psychological causes are known. Besides, the particular diagnosis may imply some specific approaches (*e.g.*, a diagnosis of minimal brain-injury may suggest the need for structure).

In addition to the overall attitude of the classroom teacher toward the handicapped child in his classroom, there are specific techniques which can serve to develop a positive self-image.

USE OF SUCCESS-ASSURED ACTIVITIES. Failure breeds failure in that it often creates attitudes and fears which militate further against learning (Riessman 1962: 86). For the child who has constantly experienced scorn, rebuffs and failure, school experiences that offer him a high probability of success are essential (Rhodes 1966: 408; Haring and Whelan 1966: 397). It may even be necessary for the teacher to start below the child's supposed level of achievement (Harper and Wright 1962: 366). The selection of tailor-made class assignments, while difficult to achieve in the regular classroom, is not impossible. Teaching by groups and the unit method are two approaches that lend themselves to individualization.

ASSIGNMENT OF SPECIAL TASKS. All children like to feel that they are important. A handicapped child in a regular classroom is often bypassed as the various "monitorships" are assigned. His self-esteem is enhanced if he, too, is given a special job to do (distributing materials, caring for the plants, running errands, collecting milk money, emptying wastepaper baskets). This shows that the teacher has confidence in him and increases the aura of his "normalcy" for the class as well as for the child himself.

Care should be taken, in the assignment of special jobs, that negative stereotypes are not reinforced. For example, a mildly retarded child in a regular classroom may be physically strong. The teacher should avoid assigning him solely "brawn" tasks; an occasional assignment such as filing cards, looking up phone numbers or operating a motion-picture projector can enhance his self-image as a "learner."

USE OF PRAISE. The child who customarily fails school tasks is starved for positive "feedbacks." Handicapped children often have strengths in some areas (Gray 1962: 265), and an effective educational program considers not only their problems but their conflict-free areas as well (Peter 1965: 11). Even small signs of growth should be recognized; these, however, should be genuinely praiseworthy so as to avoid giving the child (and his classmates) the idea that the teacher expects very little from him.

It is important for the teacher to know what the child can do and what he cannot do; he is then in a position to call on him when he thinks he will succeed and, conversely, to avoid calling on him in instances where the failure probability is high. Praise can take many forms: verbal expressions, gestures, displaying written work on the bulletin board, letting the child show (or read) his work to another class, a note to his parents, etc.

Theorists often regard learning and behavior problems as examples of maladaptive behavior—*i.e.*, the individual, via stimulus-response associations, has *learned* to cope with school tasks and interpersonal relationships in a faulty manner (Ullmann and Krasner 1965: 1–67; Haring and Whelan 1962: 389–405). The implication is clear: Learned maladaptive behavior can be "unlearned" (*i.e.*, extinguished), and more appropriate environmental intercourse can be created and nurtured via reinforcement. The use of meaningful praise, therefore, is not only intuitively correct, in consonance with the belief of mental hygienists; seen as reinforcement, it bears the edict of learning theorists as well.

AVOIDING VALUE JUDGMENTS. Teachers are becoming more conversant with psychological considerations and are generally aware of the phenomenon of nonverbal communication; *i.e.*, many teachers feel that "it is not so much *what* we say as *how* we say it" that determines the essence of the message transmitted to the child. However, it seems reasonable to expect that a child's self-concept may depend to some extent on the sheer content of the message. For example, if a teacher tells a mildly cerebral palsied child to "use your good hand," and even if she says it in a warm, friendly tone, does it not nevertheless convey to the child (and his classmates) that his other hand is a "bad" one? Wouldn't it have been more appropriate to refer simply to "left hand" and "right hand"? Similarly, instead of labeling a brain-injured child's impulsivity as "rudeness," might it not be more effective to say, "You remembered our rule much better yesterday and I'm sure that if you try, you'll be just as good at it today"? Clearly, it is less threatening to an emotionally disturbed child to have his immature penmanship referred to as "a little on the large size" instead of "sloppy" or "scribbling." Children (especially those whose egos are already fragile because of failure and lack of acceptance) are likely to be affected by negative value judgments; a positive attitude is one that encompasses both the content of the message as well as the manner of delivery. Both are products of the teacher's own attitude toward the child, but the former (*i.e.*, choosing the correct words) is a knack that can be developed through awareness and effort.

DIRECT APPEAL TO THE OTHER MEMBERS OF THE CLASS. It is often said that children are cruel. It is certainly true that children who manifest learning or behavior problems often encounter teasing and bullying from their "normal" classmates. There is, however, another side of the coin: Children can also be loving and kind. What is needed is leadership and example (Siegel 1967: 357). The teacher, by accepting the handicapped child, establishes the model.

In addition, the teacher can actually make direct appeals to the rest of the class; this is best accomplished when the handicapped child (or children) is not in the room. The appeal should not be made in medical or psychological terms, but merely state the fact that here is a child; these are his problems; *they are not due to willfulness;* these are his strengths; and we can help him in these ways.

In some cases, less direct methods of effecting peer acceptance may prove effective. These might include forums, discussion groups, group guidance lessons, "psychology" lessons, bibliotherapy (selection of pertinent literature which might afford insight into feelings) and social studies, with emphasis on the democratic ideals pertaining to the rights, value and dignity of the individual.

Anxiety

Authorities recognize that some degree of anxiety serves as a motivational spur, and that children who lack all anxiety (sociopaths) encounter considerable difficulty in the learning process (Krippner 1963: 259). However, children with learning and/or behavior problems are often *besieged* with anxiety. Retarded children can be plagued with doubts, failure and rejection centering about their inability to render satisfactory performances (Jordan 1962: 159). Emotionally disturbed children frequently have a "general pervasive mood of unhappiness or depression." (Bower and Lambert 1965: 129). Many writers (Krupp and Schwartzberg 1960; Beck 1961: 58; Bradley 1955: 90–91) agree that the minimally brain-injured generally suffer anxiety. This anxiety may be a result of frustration, inability to perceive the environment reliably (and a consequent substandard performance) and rejection by the public at large.

Certain negative cycles ensue: (1) The anxiety of the parents is often fed by—and subsequently feeds into—the anxiety of these children (Bradley 1955: 91). (2) Not only is anxiety caused by poor performance but, in turn, it may cause even lower performance. Bower (1962: 612) reminds us that even normal subjects who are suffering just a moderate degree of free-floating anxiety lose much of their ability to remember specifics such as telephone numbers and street addresses and are not able to reason to full capacity.

Plainly, there is a direct relationship between poor performance and anxiety, with one being both the cause and effect of the other, self-concept acting as the mediator. A knowledgeable and talented teacher, aware of the nature and needs of the learning and/or behaviorally impaired, can be instrumental in breaking this negative cycle.

CHOOSE "FAILURE-FREE" ACTIVITIES. Very often, children who have repeatedly experienced failure (and hence, rejection) are afraid to perform, lest they give the "wrong answer" again. To overcome this problem, the teacher can select activities in which there are no wrong or right answers (*e.g.,* What does this music make you think of? What season do you like best? Why? How do you think this story will end?).

USE ACTIVITIES CAREFULLY GRADED IN DEGREES OF "SUCCESS ASSURANCE." In the beginning, children suffering from failure-induced anxiety need activities in which they are bound to succeed. Only gradually, as the child learns to cope with some failure, should they be increased in complexity.

USE SHORT DOSES OF ACTIVITY. It is generally agreed that a child's attention span is inversely proportional to the anxiety he is experiencing—that is, his attention span is shortened when he is anxious and, conversely, lengthened when he is relaxed (Barsch 1965: 333, 334). Modification is the key word here: A half page of silent reading may be more desirable than a whole page; two arithmetic problems may be better than four; three lines of penmanship may be recommended in lieu of an entire page, and so on.

The teacher's knowledge of the child's fatigability is crucial to the development of positive teacher-child relationships. For example, a child's penmanship efforts might resemble this:

A cursory glance at this work sample "proves" to the teacher that the child could do better if only he wanted to: After all, the child who scribbled at the end of the line is the same child who demonstrated acceptable penmanship at the beginning. Even if the teacher questions such a child about his scribbling, he may well answer, "I wanted to." This seemingly devil-may-care attitude often masks deep feelings of inadequacy; it is safer (*i.e.*, less painful) for the child to feign nonchalance than to admit a basic inferiority.

The knowledgeable teacher, perceiving the real reason behind the discrepancy in performance, can embark on a course to help the child increase his temporal tolerance.

USE TIMED EXPERIENCES SPARINGLY. Often the knowledge that his performance is being timed heightens a child's feelings of anxiety. Some children (particularly the culturally deprived) are not time-oriented and require a somewhat leisurely pace—the additional time requirement not signifying mental retardation but reflecting elements of a different style: patience, care, planning, desire to mull things over, etc. (Riessman 1962: 65–66). If at all possible, the classroom teacher should make allowances for these children during activities which are normally timed—*e.g.*, he could allow additional time for class tests and assign *optional* work to those who finish early. In this way, the pressure of time is diminished, since those who require more time are not penalized.

USE OF PUPPETRY. Puppetry is recommended for many reasons. To begin with, mildly handicapped children in the regular classroom are painfully aware of the difference between themselves and the nonhandicapped children around them. They may become overly sensitive, fearful of reciting, avoiding eye contact and shrinking from any role that might place them in the limelight. By means of puppets, such children are able, without fear, to satisfy the natural need to be the center of attention, for the audience watches the puppet rather than the child. Fluency can often be promoted even with stutterers (who may be extremely self-conscious regarding their speech) by means of talking through puppets (Lent 1962: 329).

Woltman (1966: 202-8) lists additional reasons for using puppets: (1) There is a close interaction between the audience and the puppet in a hand puppet show. (2) Puppetry is a projective technique (the performer, through puppets, can project the core of his fears and anxieties; this opportunity to air his feelings in a socially acceptable way helps the child while simultaneously supplying the teacher with additional information about him).

UTILIZE ACTIVITIES THAT DIMINISH PREOCCUPATION WITH SELF. It is quite common for children who perceive themselves as different from (hence, inferior to) their peers to become preoccupied with themselves. One of the major characteristics of the life style of neurotics is a "preoccupation with personal problems to the exclusion of any outside interests" (Landis and Bolles 1947: 87). A brain-injured child's faulty communication pattern—speaking only about himself, not checking to see if his audience is listening, etc.—is often related to egocentricity of language and thought (Strauss and Kephart 1955: 94-96). Finally, the mentally retarded child, being less mature socially and intellectually than his nonhandicapped counterpart, may be at an egocentric (rather than the more mature sociocentric) stage of development.

There are some ways in which a regular classroom teacher can help the handicapped children in his class become less preoccupied with themselves and, reciprocally, more sociocentric (*i.e.*, more concerned and aware of others) :

Games: Most games are fun, and playing them can be relaxing. This feeling of relaxation (*i.e.*, diminished tension and anxiety) makes it less necessary for the child to be overly concerned with himself. Moreover, games frequently require some *group* effort, thereby promoting sociocentric thinking.

Humor: Tension can often be reduced by the injection of humor. In addition, humor can foster motivation and can help sustain interest. Funny songs, humorous stories, as well as the situational use of humor can be employed. Humor—by definition pleasurable and nonthreatening—can demonstrate to the children the teacher's warmth, good-naturedness and accepting attitude, and can also promote "groupness" inasmuch as the class as a whole shares the humorous situation.

"Therapeutic" activities: Activities such as creative writing, discussion, group "guidance" classes, play therapy, impromptu skits, etc., can create an acceptable way for the child who is preoccupied with himself to air some of his personal problems. Projective techniques including bibliotherapy (*i.e.*, the careful selection of stories which permit the children to express viewpoints about—and understand—*themselves,* while ostensibly discussing the story) can be beneficial.

It is important that the teacher develop insight into the nature and needs (including ego strength) of his pupils. Just as these projective techniques might be useful in some situations, they might be contraindicated in others; in such instances, the teacher would use neutralization—*i.e.,* the removal of emotionally threatening subject matter from teaching materials and methods (Jacobson and Faegre 1959: 243–46).

Helping others: The handicapped child in the regular classroom should be encouraged to help others. He might be able to tutor (drill or explain some point) to a classmate in some area in which he excels; time could be set aside for him to help younger children in lower classes by playing with them, reading to them, etc. (many of the learning and/or behavior problem children relate well with younger children) ; he might even be asked to help outside the school (volunteer work in hospitals or community centers, for example) .

This interest in others tends to diminish the handicapped child's preoccupation with himself while simultaneously proving to him that he has some areas of strength; it also increases the number of social contacts and, in this way, tends to promote social maturity.

Difficulty in Paying Attention

Obviously, learning cannot occur until the student's attention is engaged. Retardates often learn at an even slower rate than would be expected by virtue of their mental age, and it is very likely that this discrepancy is due to problems of attention (Zeaman and House 1963: 159) . A major characteristic of brain-injured children is an inability to focus their attention readily on the foreground, that is, on the task at hand. Anxiety, preoccupation with personal problems, an inability to control intruding thoughts and fantasizing are frequently at the root of the inattentiveness of many emotionally disturbed children. Cultural deprivation, often a causal factor of mental retardation (Sarason 1959: 464–529) and linked with many cases of social and emotional maladjustment (Black 1966: 45–50; Clark 1962: 460–5; Frost and Hawkes 1966: 1–10) , also impinges upon the child's ability to attend in several specific ways. The culturally deprived may simply have inferior *habits* of hearing, seeing and thinking because their environment did not *teach* them to pay attention to the essence of what is being said or of what is happening (Havighurst 1966: 19); then, too, their values, attitudes and interests are not in consonance with the middle-class mores reflected in the materials, curriculum, methods and teachers encountered in school (Riessman 1962).

Listed below are some practical suggestions that might assist a regular classroom teacher in dealing with the attention problem of minimally handicapped children:

REDUCE EXTRANEOUS STIMULI. Many children, particularly the brain-damaged, are inattentive because extraneous stimuli compete for their attention; they are bombarded by various sensory data and cannot readily filter out what is unimportant. This is especially true of *proximal* stimuli. Hence, desks and immediate surroundings should be clear of pens, pencils, notices, previous activities' materials, gloves, rings and other "seductive" objects. Boots, raincoats, briefcases, lunch boxes, etc., should be some distance from the child. These are desirable routines for the entire class—for the normal majority as well as for the handicapped few. The teacher might remind the inattentive child to clear his desk or he might assign a "buddy" to help him. Needless to say, all reminding, assistance and enforcing of a rule for an individual should be done in an accepting, unobtrusive, supportive manner.

KEEP UNSTRUCTURED TIME TO A MINIMUM. The inattentive child is most likely to be inattentive during transitions, idle periods, unstructured time. Following a few simple routines, the classroom teacher can keep these periods to a minimum:

1. *Distribute materials quickly.* It is not necessary to let each student choose material during distribution. For example, if the teacher walks up and down the aisle instructing each child to choose three crayons from a large container of crayons, an inordinate amount of time is wasted, and listlessness and inattention follow. It is much more effective simply to distribute them as quickly as possible without inviting deliberation.

2. *Alternate performers.* It isn't necessary for *each* child to have to watch—or listen to—every other child render the same

performance. If, for pedagogical purposes, the teacher finds it necessary to hear each child recite, this should be spread over several class days, alternating performers, so as, finally, to give each child an opportunity to recite or perform.

3. *Ask Prodding Questions.* When one child is performing (*e.g.*, reciting, answering a question orally, writing an example on the blackboard, etc.), the teacher should encourage the other children to attend: "Do you think he'll get it right?"; "Will you agree with him?"; "Did you do your example the same way?" This gentle prodding to attend diminishes lethargy and increases interest.

MAKE SURE PERTINENT VISUAL STIMULI CAN BE SEEN. All children must be seated so that they will be able to see the blackboard, charts, the performer, etc. Charts and lettering on the blackboard should be sufficiently large and correctly formed. If a child is standing while reciting he must not block the view of those in their seats.

EMPLOY VARIETY. Change, per se, can stimulate attention. Each lesson should include a meaningful variety of activities. These should be cohesive and sequential. Tempo changes and small doses are beneficial for children who have problems in attending. The teacher should avoid relying solely on *talking* activities (questions and answers, discussion, lecture) and should include *doing* (*e.g.*, silent reading, brief written exercises, dictionary work, sorting, matching, pasting, coloring and construction) activities as well. Also, distal-proximal changes can increase the child's attention. For example, the child should have experience working with materials that are on his desk as well as with materials that are more distant from him; similarly, the teacher should at times be next to the inattentive child as he speaks to the class, and at other times be across the room from him.

KEEP TEACHER'S VERBALISM TO A MINIMUM. Brain-injured children often have auditory perceptual impairment and are not able to tolerate nor decipher massive doses of words as the teacher gives instructions, explanations and descriptions. Similarly, culturally deprived children are frequently bewildered by teachers' excessive verbalism inasmuch as their background has not sufficiently rehearsed them in maintaining auditory attention to adult speech (Riessman 1962: 84). The classroom teacher, by speaking more slowly, less frequently, in small doses and by simplifying verbal instructions, will be helping the inattentive child learn to listen.

SEAT QUIET, WITHDRAWN CHILDREN NEAR THE "ACTION." Many emotionally disturbed children feel anxious, insecure and inadequate; consequently, they withdraw from the mainstream and indulge in fantasy; similarly, brain-injured children, although "stimulus-bound" are often distracted by proximal stimuli—hence, they have a tendency to fidget and to manipulate objects on their desks while ignoring the task at hand, which may be some distance from them. Often, a seat change, placing them nearer the "action" (more active members of the class, the blackboard, the teacher's desk, the performer, etc.), can serve to direct their attention in the proper channels.

MAKE PROVISIONS FOR PHYSICAL MOVEMENT. Sitting for long, uninterrupted periods of time often creates boredom, listlessness, fatigue and inattention. The purely physical advantages of injecting movement into an otherwise completely sedentary experience are well known: *e.g.*, standing and taking deep breaths of air increases the oxygen intake; the baseball game's "seventh-inning stretch" invigorates cramped muscles and increases circulation; a theater's intermission period can provide the time for additional physical relief (stretching, walking, talking, using bathroom, relieving thirst, etc.).

Besides these basically physical reasons for providing for individual mobility, science has recently pointed out that active movement tends to improve sensory-perceptual interpretation. Freedman and others (1961: 60–61) cite sensory deprivation experiments in which subjects, experiencing prism-induced disarrangement, could not achieve visual accommodation unless allowed to move actively; that is, the prisms caused visual distortions; these did not disappear even when the subjects were wheeled in a wheelchair over a given route; the distortion disappeared only when the subjects were allowed to walk the route. Similarly, hallucinations caused by voluntary sensory deprivation persevered when motility was restricted, but were minimal or disappeared under free motility conditions.

A compelling implication emerges: Might not some of the perceptual distortions of the brain-injured child be minimized through motility? Similarly, might not active physical movement diminish the daydreams, fantasies and possible hallucinations of an emotionally disturbed child?

There are many ways in which the astute teacher can provide for the motility of the inattentive child: changing seats for group work; letting the child do some work at the blackboard; getting, distributing and collecting materials; errands, etc.

In general, teachers of young children provide opportunities for the children to move (namely, the common "stretching and deep-breathing" periods, the Simon Says games, the finger-play songs, etc.). The teacher of older children, in meaningful and appropriate ways, can also during the classroom lesson include occasions for children, particularly the inattentive ones, to move.

UTILIZE SPECIFIC LISTENING TRAINING. Many children have never really learned to listen, but there are activities that can foster this skill.

The elementary teacher can play such games as Guess the Voice, Magic Music (in which he directs a child's movement toward a hidden object by varying the volume of his piano playing), identifying sounds, Name the Tune, reproducing long-short clapping patterns, etc. In addition, storytelling, drama, music appreciation, auditory discrimination in phonics, all demand purposeful listening.

Teachers of older children can also train them to listen. Some games such as What's My Line?, Twenty Questions and Pass

Word are appropriate as well as motivating. In addition, such activities as debates, oral reporting and telephone skills development can be useful in providing listening experiences.

Audio aids such as tape recorders, phonographs and radios can be beneficial, too.

In listening training (as in all effective teaching) a sequential approach is imperative: first, short doses, then larger doses; first, simple activities, then more complex ones.

PLAN CLASSROOM EXPERIENCES THAT ARE INTERESTING. Any child, regardless of his diagnosis, will be more likely to pay attention if he finds the subject matter, the manner of presentation and the particular activity interesting. There are many ways in which the regular classroom teacher can provide experiences that are of interest to all children—including those who are inattentive.

Be aware of children's backgrounds. A teacher's personal attitudes, values and interests, being functions of his own socioeconomic background (usually middle class), may not be in consonance with those of the pupils in his class. This is especially true in the case of culturally disadvantaged children (Riessman 1962; Haubrich 1966: 362–68) and has implications in all grades, even as early as kindergarten. For example, Gotkin (1967: 406–17) states that lower-class children probably do not experience and perceive the passage of time in the same ways as do middle-class children because of (1) the relative lack of long-range goals in this group, and (2) its concrete and stereotyped language. They have a strong present-oriented sense of time and may have difficulty viewing time as a continuum or in extending time beyond the immediate into either the past or future. Consequently, Gotkin proposes that a seven-day calendar beginning with Saturday and Sunday, the two nonschool days, is the logical first step in a "calendar curriculum" for culturally disadvantaged children.

A child will more likely be drawn toward learning if the teacher discovers his interests and can center the lesson—or some

SAT.	SUN.	MON.	TUES.	WED.	THURS.	FRI.

aspect of the lesson—around this interest. For example, a disinterested child may be motivated toward the study of arithmetical formulae if the teacher, knowing of his interest in basketball, presents the scoring rules of that game as a formula: $P = F + 2g$, where $P =$ the total number of points, $F =$ the number of successful foul shots, and $g =$ the number of baskets (other than foul shots) completed.

Interest often coincides with needs. Kreuter (1965) shows how the needs (and therefore the interests) of emotionally disturbed adolescents can be utilized in structuring an effective curriculum: A New York City correctional institution at Riker's Island housed a male population of youthful offenders, sixteen to twenty-one years of age, misdemeanants and felons. Their areas of commonalities were chronic truancy, lack of interest in school learning, vocational aimlessness and severe academic retardation. Interest in reading was stimulated by using adult education materials—tabloids, comic books, song sheets, trade manuals and application blanks. The arithmetic curriculum used the commissary, the various shops (*e.g.*, measurement in the carpentry and tailor shops, seasonal time concepts in the greenhouse, etc.) and even the length of the inmate's sentence!

Because of the occasional grade retention of slow learners, their chronological ages are often somewhat greater than those of normal children (Johnson 1963: 141). It is generally recommended that the teacher consider this child's chronological age rather than his mental age as he tries to select material suitable for him—hence, the chronic search for high-interest/low-reading-level materials.

USE A "GAME" FORMAT. The interest of a lesson is often enhanced by employing a game situation. Riessman (1962: 71) believes that this appeals to all children, but especially to the culturally deprived child because "apparently it is related to their down-to-earth spontaneous approach to things. Their extra-verbal communication (motoric, visual) is usually called forth in games, most of which are not word-bound. Also, most games . . . are person centered and generally are concerned with direct action and visible results. Games are usually sharply defined and structured with clear-cut goals. The rules are definite and can be readily absorbed. The deprived child enjoys the challenge of the game and feels he can 'do' it; this is in sharp contrast to many verbal tasks."

The use of games in a regular classroom can benefit the mildly retarded child also inasmuch as games frequently employ repetitiveness, definitiveness and simple vocabulary.

Rhodes (1966: 405-10) feels that it is imperative that the curriculum of the emotionally disturbed child contain surroundings that excite such positive motivation as adventure, conquest, achievement, mastery and explanation. Many games do just this.

Some teachers may equate game activities with permissiveness and lack of limits and may fear the possibility of the inducement of high levels of excitement. Upon reflection, however, it seems evident that games are usually based on well-defined rules, clear and attainable goals, structure, definitiveness and cohesiveness. Seen in this light, many minimally brain-injured children can benefit by partaking in them.

The effective regular classroom teacher who endeavors to help minimally handicapped students will utilize the game format but will choose games purposefully. He will also be aware of the specific variables inherent in game activities. (Long *et al.* 1966: 414) : *e.g.,* the amount of body contact, body mobility, complexity of rules, skill requirements, degree of luck and use of props. Role-taking factors (captain, pitcher, "It") are of special significance. The individual who is "It" in a game of tag is pitted *against* the group, whereas the "Leader" in Follow the Leader has a more psychologically positive role.

USE THE UNIT-METHOD APPROACH. Teaching by units has been advocated for slow-learning children (Johnson 1963) and for emotionally disturbed children (Rhodes 1966: 408). Traditionally, educators have suggested that at least some classroom teaching adapt the unit approach since the unit (1) grows out of life situations (thereby rendering school experiences more meaningful to the child), (2) can develop social skills as well as subject matter mastery and (3) integrates the various subject areas instead of reinforcing artificial boundaries.

In addition, this method seems ideally suited to the education of the exceptional child in the regular classroom inasmuch as:

(1) A wide range of abilities, interests and needs can be accommodated by a carefully chosen unit. (2) The unit method lends itself readily to individual remedial instruction periods. (3) It allows the child who is less capable academically to achieve status by performing some nonacademic duties. (4) It fosters goal-directed activities. (5) It provides for physical mobility. (6) It fosters learning by "doing."
(7) It can be inherently interesting and motivating, and (8) it can tend to create a feeling of solidarity and mutual acceptance among the handicapped child and his normal classmates.

Difficulty in Organizing

The minimally handicapped child with learning or behavioral problems who is enrolled in a regular classroom frequently presents a rather discouraging picture of disorganization. Books, homework and special assignments such as book reports are frequently forgotten; he has a tendency to be slow in gathering his belongings and moving on to the next room (this is particularly apparent in the upper grades departmental programs); and, frequently, it is difficult for him to keep his belongings together and his desk cleared. An understanding of the nature and needs of children classified as minimal brain-injured, mentally retarded or emotionally disturbed, however, does indeed lead one to expect such disorganization. A mentally retarded child may have difficulty following instructions and understanding rules. A brain-injured child often finds it difficult to structure patterns; moreover, he frequently perseverates, and so has a tendency to be rigid and an inability to shift readily from one situation to another. An emotionally disturbed child is usually anxious, feels inadequate and may harbor negative feelings toward school—all of which can create a disorganized manner of response and action.

There follow some ways in which a regular classroom teacher can help such children become more organized:

ASSIGN A "BUDDY" TO THE DISORGANIZED CHILD. A more mature classmate can be assigned the job of helping a disorganized child "get with it" more. He can remind the child to clear his desk, to gather his belongings, to lock his gymnasium locker (lest his gym uniform be misappropriated, contributing further to the child's feelings of inadequacy). Again, the help should be given in a friendly, accepting and unobtrusive manner.

WORK MORE CLOSELY WITH PARENTS. A teacher of such children should work in close relationship with their parents. The parents should be notified of the book schedule (*i.e.*, which books are needed and when), the homework scheduling and the due date of special projects such as book reports. In this way, the parents can reinforce the teacher's efforts, and the child will be better equipped to organize himself in relation to the instructions and systems of his particular class and school.

STRUCTURE CLASSROOM PROCEDURES. There is a need for clarity and consistency in classroom procedures. Routines should be established as early as possible. The teacher should ascertain that the children understand the rules, instructions and procedures. The child's ability to organize is largely related to the degree of success the teacher has in capturing his attention.

UTILIZE TWO SETS OF BOOKS. Often, children live some distance from the school and have heavy loads of books to carry. This is particularly true of departmental programs where the teacher of one subject is unaware of the "book-carrying" requirements of the other teachers. If a child is disorganized and, in addition, somewhat clumsy (as many of these children are), he is likely often to fail to bring all the required books to school and have them arrive in good condition. A possible solution is to allow such a child to have a second set of books in school, thus eliminating the need of home-to-school book transportation. This procedure has aided physically handicapped students (cardiac, certain orthopedically handicapped, etc.) whose condition limits their ability to carry numbers of books.

As the disorganized child shows progress in overcoming his problem, he can be encouraged to carry his books again. This should be done sequentially—a little at first, more as time goes on.

A GOOD MENTAL HYGIENE APPROACH IS ESSENTIAL. As with many of the undesirable traits of these children, disorganization is often a function of their anxiety and self-deprecating feelings. The teacher, by understanding and accepting these children, by praising them for even small signs of growth in the area of organization and by striving to maintain a tension-free classroom climate, can successfully assist the child in diminishing his disorganization.

Difficulty in Copying Written Material

Children presenting learning and/or behavior problems often encounter difficulty in writing: The brain-injured child may evidence dysgraphia; this is a visuo-motor impairment in which the child is greatly hindered in his attempts to translate what he sees (letters, words, etc.) into motor patterns (Johnson and Myklebust 1967: 199–202). A mentally retarded child, being below average in incidental learning abilities, may find it difficult to master penmanship if it is taught only tangentially (as an integrated skill) rather than specifically (Enstrom 1966: 385).

Particularly troublesome to these children is the task of copying written material from the blackboard to their papers. Two factors that contribute to this difficulty are the vertical-to-horizontal plane translation and the distance between the two surfaces.

It is not uncommon to find a minimally brain-injured child in a regular junior high school or high school class who fails test after test in a given subject, not because he does not know that subject but simply because he cannot copy large amounts of blackboard material quickly. Here are some modifications that the classroom teacher can make to remedy this situation:

A. Use a duplicating machine (rexograph, hectograph, ditto, spirit duplicator, etc.) to make copies of written material such as tests and homework assignments.

B. Allow a "buddy" to make a carbon copy of his work for the handicapped student.

C. Require less copying. For example, suppose an English test requires the class to copy ten sentences *and* to draw a ring around each noun; the slow writer could be instructed to simply *list* each noun.

D. The young child who is learning to copy from the blackboard to the paper on his desk may need remedial help. The teacher may do this himself, recommend private tutoring or instruct the parent in how to give the child practice periods of writing at home.

Sequence is the key here: (1) Small doses precede larger ones. (2) Copying from a book (or paper) which is on the child's desk alongside his own work precedes copying from a blackboard. (3) The distance between the blackboard and the child's work should be increased gradually. (4) The size of the blackboard work should be sufficiently large, especially in the beginning. (5) A tiltboard may serve effectively as a mediator between the completely vertical plane of the blackboard and the completely horizontal plane of the desk.

Not only is sequence important in helping a child learn to copy from the blackboard; it is an important educational principal in the overall area of remedial handwriting. Some examples of a sequential approach in the remediation of handwriting skills follow:

1. Guiding the child's hand is a first step toward independent writing. Other preliminary activities are tracing and connecting dots.
2. Copying precedes writing from dictation which, in turn, precedes writing creatively.
3. The writing of single letters precedes the writing of words.
4. Manuscript writing generally precedes cursive writing.
5. Double-spaced lines precede single-spaced lines.
6. Lined paper precedes unlined paper.
7. There is a correct sequence for teaching letters, not simply alphabetically (for example, in cursive writing, l, e, t, i should be taught first, before the more complicated letters).
8. Letter strokes should be carefully taught in correct sequence (Enstrom, 1966: 386).

E. Writing "freehand" is often hard for these children, for a brain-injured or mentally retarded child may have faulty visual perception and subsequent poor spatial orientation and an emotionally disturbed child may literally need limits. Ruling of lines by the teacher often helps these children with heights of letters, spacing and in writing "straight," *i.e.*, without rotation. Special commercial penmanship paper is available, which even has the half-space line lightly drawn in, thereby facilitating the differentiation between the height of the large letters and that of the small letters.

F. Offer structure and support. In many instances, poor penmanship and difficulty in copying are part of an overall disorganization syndrome: poor work habits, disorderly and disarranged notebook, poor personal hygiene habits, unsharpened pencil and smudgy eraser, etc. The teacher can support the child by helping him structure his surroundings (keeping desk uncluttered; bringing correct materials to school and leaving extraneous supplies at home; starting to write on time, avoiding dawdling, etc.). A supportive attitude on the part of the teacher has psychological values as well: Acceptance leads to greater self-esteem, which, in turn, can lead to pride in appearance and belongings.

G. Finally, older children who continue to experience difficulty in penmanship should be encouraged to learn typewriting, not as a substitute for writing but as an additional skill—one that can facilitate learning in the broad area of language arts.

Poor Coordination

Most (if not all) minimally brain-injured children present some kind of coordination problems. This may be a manifestation of a mild cerebral palsy (motor impairment due to brain injury) or a direct result of perceptual dysfunctioning. Some common examples of such incoordination are difficulty in dressing, problems in arts and crafts, poor handwriting, general sloppiness, lack of mechanical ability and inability to master athletics readily at any level—from skipping and hopping to playing baseball.

In addition to the brain-injured, the slow learners, as a group, also demonstrate incoordination (Johnson 1963: 30–1). Oddly, some emotionally disturbed children share this problem. This may be a result of (1) perceptual distortion, especially faulty body image (2) feelings of anxiety and self-consciousness, which hinder their performance (3) their lack of acceptance—and, therefore, lack of experience—in group games, or (4) actual brain damage (Cohn and Nardini 1958).

Here are some ways in which a regular classroom teacher can help children who have problems in coordination.

EMPLOY SEQUENTIALIZED EXPERIENCES. Obviously, these children need to participate in a variety of physical activities. However, these should be well-planned; sequence is just as important in physical education, arts and crafts, and shop as it is in the more academic subject areas. Sequence, here, has a variety of dimensions.

1. Many incoordinative children, particularly young ones, are afraid to play ball. Because of their poor spatial orientation and visual imperception, they may find it difficult to judge the speed of an approaching ball, often perceiving a faster speed; they flinch, close their eyes, shield their faces with their hands as a thrown ball approaches them. Teachers can often help these children by letting them play with a balloon first (a balloon is lighter than a ball; it always approaches the catcher slowly; it is fun to play with and, unlike a ball, doesn't hurt even if it strikes the child). After successful experiences with balloons, the child is ready to move to *large* rubber balls (beach balls, volley balls, etc.) and then to smaller rubber balls. A beanbag can also be used as an intermediate step.

Similarly, catching a ball that is rolled along the floor should precede catching a thrown ball. The correct sequence is: rolled ball, bounced ball, thrown ball.

2. Simple, whole-body activities are prerequisites to the development of more complicated skills such as those demanded in basketball or baseball. Frostig and Horne (1964: 21–26) suggest four areas of gross motor coordinating exercises:*

> (a) Regaining an upright position (children sit on the floor, knees bent, then get up; children lie on the floor, then get up; children make rhythmic jumps in the air, making quarter-turns, then half-turns and finally full turns, while jumping, etc.).
>
> (b) Locomotor activities (crawling forward, backward and sideways; skipping, galloping, hopping, etc.).
>
> (c) Imaginative games (one child who is the "horse" pulls another child who is the "cart," the "cart" holding the "horse" around the waist; children move forward, or backward, pretend-

* Used with permission from *The Frostig Program for the Development of Visual Perception: Teacher's Guide* (Chicago, Follet Educational Corporation, 1964).

ing to pull or push a load; children pantomime trees, airplanes, birds, rabbits, etc.).

(d) Balancing (use of balance board, standing on tiptoe, standing on one leg, etc.).

Dunsing and Kephart (1965: 89) stress the importance of balance, pointing out that balancing:

> involves a smoothly coordinated control of muscles in relation to each other. In order to balance himself effectively, the child must not only know where his center of gravity is, but he must be flexible enough so that he can easily move around it without fear of falling. If he is not able to do this, he cannot explore his environment. He cannot interrelate with objects because he cannot move out of a tightly restricted relationship which preserves a tenuous relationship to gravity.

These activities would seem to be inherently more interesting to younger rather than older children, but a resourceful gym teacher of older children (junior high or even high school) can incorporate some of these activities in a calisthenics or body-building program.

3. Because gross motor development precedes fine motor development, it is not uncommon to find children who, although they may scribble and have great difficulty in pasting, coloring, tracing (or, if they are older children, in typing, shop work, ball playing), still demonstrate at least adequate ability in swimming or bicycle riding.

Sequential training should first provide for large muscle activities; then gradually, in small doses carefully graded in complexity, introduce experiences that rely on fine motor coordination. Knowledge of this sequential development has implication in all grade levels—*e.g.,* the secondary school teacher should realize that the cooking program of a homemaking course does not require as much fine muscle skill as does sewing; similarly, using a hammer in a woodworking shop does not require the finger dexterity that soldering small components in the electric shop does.

PROVIDE VISUAL PERCEPTUAL TRAINING. Incoordination is often a result of visual perceptual deficits. Perceptual training in the classroom can frequently facilitate a more adequate motor functioning.

Frostig and Horne (1964: 18–21) suggest certain eye-movement exercises:*

1. Left-right progression. Children try to focus their eyes—without turning their heads—on an object moving from left to right (*e.g.*, a ball rolling or a toy moving across a tabletop) ; the recommended distance between the moving object and the viewer is about five feet.

2. Peripheral vision stimulation. The child, while standing, is told to stare straight ahead at some fixed point; the teacher, from a distance of about 20 inches in front of the child, slowly moves an object, starting at the extremes of the child's peripheral vision, toward his line of sight. The object is moved until it is recognized, and continues in motion until the child reports that it is out of sight. The objects (*e.g.*, beads, small toys, cardboard pictures) should be alternated to insure identification rather than memorization.

3. Focusing eyes with head in motion (this skill is necessary in many athletic activities). An object is held stationary in front of the child, who must focus on it while moving his head up and down, side to side, or even (for brief periods) in a rolling motion.

4. Focusing eyes with head held stationary. Three vertical columns of numbers or words are written on the blackboard; the child, with head held stationary, moves his focus from the symbol in the left column to the respective one in the middle and right columns.

* Used with permission from *The Frostig Program for the Development of Visual Perception: Teacher's Guide* (Chicago, Follett Educational Corporation, 1964).

5. Following regular movements (*e.g.*, an object tied to a piece of string as it swings in pendulum fashion, a piece of chalk as regular shapes—circles, squares, spirals, etc.—are drawn at the blackboard) and following irregular movements (*e.g.*, a piece of chalk as it draws irregular patterns at the blackboard, a moving flashlight beam, etc.).

Visual perceptual problems are related not only to incoordination but to learning difficulties as well. In a sample of 89 children nine years of age or older who had learning difficulties of such magnitude that they were referred to an educational clinic, 78 percent had visual perceptual disturbances (Frostig and Horne, 1964: 12). Problems in visual perception are fairly common, particularly among young children: Frostig and Horne (1964: 13) state that 20 to 25 percent of children being enrolled in the first grade "lack the necessary perceptual maturity to succeed in beginning reading, arithmetic and writing without putting forth undue effort." Seen in this light, a visual perceptual training program in the regular classroom seeks to benefit the mildly handicapped child *correctively* and the normal child *preventatively*.

The teacher must know how and when to include visual perceptual training in lessons. Some training can be done on a group basis, perhaps using a game format; at other times, the teacher may judiciously find some time to work with an individual or with small groups of children. He may even instruct the parent regarding some basic perceptual training in the home. In some instances, where the problem seems to be a complex one, the teacher may wish to suggest that the parent obtain the advice of a visual training specialist.

PROVIDE BODY-IMAGE ACTIVITIES. One's ability to manipulate his body through the spatial environment with agility, grace, dexterity and sure-footedness is largely dependent upon his body image. Beginning with the very early stages of development, the individual organizes his body image by integrating various sensory-perceptual data—the body image becoming impressed directly into the nervous system (Rosen 1966: 1). Brain-injured children, often suffering perceptual distortions, develop, in turn, a distorted body image. Some emotionally disturbed children also have poor body image, an extreme example being the psychotic, who, lacking psychic boundary and a sense of unity, may believe that he is more than one person, that he is fragmented into separate limbs or that others can read into his mind, since his thoughts and perceptions are outside of himself (Rosen 1966: 3). It may be that the mildly emotionally disturbed child suffers from this distortion in a lesser form.

There are various opportunities for the regular classroom teacher to employ activities which foster an ordered, reliable body-image development:

1. Games such as Simon Says and Follow the Leader can be extremely helpful. Pin the Tail on the Donkey helps the child orient himself in space. (Omit turning the child around. Simply blindfold him and let him try to find the donkey.)

2. Creative dancing, pantomime, imitation of animal movements, finger-play songs are all useful.

3. Awareness of bodies, in general, can be strengthened by letting children draw figures of people, model clay figures, assemble puzzles that depict people, arrange cloth body parts on a felt board to form the body, touch different parts of a doll's body, etc.

4. A child's awareness of his own body—physically as well as psychologically—can be enhanced by having him lie down on top of a large sheet of wrapping paper, tracing his body's outline, cutting out the paper silhouette and mounting it on the classroom wall. Games involving children's shadows are also useful.

5. Directionality and spatial orientations are closely interrelated with body image (Knickerbocker 1966: 27). Hence, activities involving directionality (left-right, up-down, behind-in front of) and spatial orientation (*e.g.,* near-far, toward-away

from, middle-end, top-bottom, relative speeds of approaching objects) can be useful.

Again, many of these activities seem more suitable to the classroom program of young children; however, older children can often be similarly helped via such activities as calisthenics, marching, dancing, sports of various kinds and some social games such as charades, etc. Even such subjects as dramatics, hygiene or biology relate to body image.

ALL ACTIVITIES AIMED AT CORRECTION (AND PREVENTION) OF INCOORDINATION SHOULD BE SATISFYING AND PLEASANT. The movement of one's own body is a highly personal affair, and one can, understandably, develop deep feelings of inferiority through inadequate motor performance, much more readily, perhaps, than in other areas. After all, if you criticize my skills in an arithmetic test, I can (albeit with some effort) regard the arithmetic paper as a product somewhat apart from myself; however, if you laugh at my hopping, skipping or throwing, clearly you are laughing at *me*.

As a coping mechanism, many children move away from situations which are associated with past unsatisfying experiences and are therefore likely to be unsatisfying or unpleasant again. Teachers can often help such youngsters overcome this aversion by introducing them gradually and at times almost coincidentally to that particular activity.

For example, some children, because of unpleasant interpersonal experiences (*e.g.*, teasing, bullying, scorn, rejection) associated with their past efforts at playing ball, refuse to engage in ball games or even in informal throwing and catching sessions. The teacher can invite the child to join him (or another child) in a game of hitting a penny with a ball (the penny is placed on a horizontal line about three feet from each player; they face each other and take turns trying to hit the penny with a rubber ball). The catching and throwing seem almost peripheral to the goal of the game, and therefore the child is not too likely to decline participation; moreover, the bouncing of the ball slows it down and makes it easier to catch.

PROGRAMS WHICH PROMOTE COORDINATION ACTIVITIES SHOULD BE ONGOING. Best results will be obtained if the visual training, visual-motor activities, body-image training and coordination activities in which the child participates in school are carried over into his extraschool program. The teacher (regular classroom, gym, shop, etc.) can often apprize other professionals (*e.g.,* camp personnel, scout leaders, social and recreational program heads, etc.) of the nature of the child's problems and the goals and methodologies of the school.

Parents (and older siblings) can also help in this respect; hence the need for positive parent-teacher relationships. Many parents, though motivated positively toward helping their handicapped children, may yet benefit from the guidance of the classroom teacher. For example, an overly ambitious father may push his child toward father-son baseball activities when actually the child's readiness stage may warrant a more elementary phase such as balloon activities or a peripheral approach such as hitting a penny with a rubber ball or even tossing pebbles into a pond or lake.

Difficulty in Abstract Thinking

It is common knowledge that abstract thinking abilities enable us to deal with symbols and ideas, whereas the concrete level necessitates our dealing with real objects—objects that can be seen, touched and manipulated (hence, two actual apples are more meaningful than the symbol "2" for the child who is at the concrete level of functioning). Besides this idea vs. object dichotomy, there are additional aspects of abstract thinking. Goldstein and Sheerer (1941: 1–8) list the following modes of behavior which characterize an abstract attitude:

(a) to detach our ego from the outerworld or from inner experience (*e.g.,* to be able to repeat—when requested by the examiner—that "the snow is black").

(b) to assume a mental set willfully and consciously (*e.g.,* to be able to recite the names of the week, serially, when interrupted at this task, without having to go back to the beginning).

(c) to account for acts to oneself or to others (*e.g.*, to describe verbally the physical steps one uses in opening a door latch).

(d) to shift reflectively from one aspect of the situation to another (*e.g.*, to shift visually from one face to another in the well-known Ruben's ambiguous face-vase drawing).

(e) to hold in mind simultaneously various aspects.

(f) to grasp the essential of a given whole; to break up a given whole into parts; to isolate and to synthesize them (*e.g.*, seeing the point of a joke or a cartoon).

(g) to abstract common properties reflectively; to form hierarchic concepts (*e.g.*, understanding analogies or metaphors; sorting objects or pictures, *i.e.*, finding the common denominator).

(h) to plan ahead ideationally (*e.g.*, to give a verbal account of a path along which one walks daily).

Strauss and Kephart (1955: 112–27) include as examples of abstract thinking the ability to discern similarities when superimposed by superficial environmental variations (*i.e.*, the ability to generalize), to deal with possibilities as well as actualities, to be aware of the existence of hidden elements in an object as we look at only those elements which meet the eye, the ability to use language so that the word demarcates and holds intact the observed conceptual similarities, the ability to manipulate past experiences freely.

Children suffering from learning and/or behavior impairment are often deficient in the ability to make abstractions. Since mental retardation is defined, in essence, as poor performance on a standardized intelligence test, and since research shows a direct relationship between problem solving and/or conceptual behavior and IQ or MA (Rosenberg 1963: 439–59) the mentally retarded child—even the minimally retarded—by definition, has impaired abstracting ability. Authorities

(Clements 1966: 11–12) generally agree that the minimally brain-injured child often has disorders of the thinking process characterized by poor ability for abstract reasoning, generally concrete thinking, difficulties in concept formation, frequently disorganized thinking, poor short-term and long-term memory, sometimes autistic thinking, frequent thought perseveration. Goldstein and Sheerer (1941: 1) point out that difficulty in thinking abstractly often accompanies brain-injury, retardation as well as schizophrenia.

Here are some suggested approaches by which the regular classroom teacher can help these children overcome some of their conceptual deficits:

USE CONCRETE MATERIALS. Very often, the child who encounters difficulty in dealing with symbols can fare better with actual objects. Arithmetic is an ideal area for the utilization of materials: *e.g.*, beads, disks, pegs, squared material for demonstrating place value, circular material (whole as well as divided) for demonstrating fractional parts. More complex arithmetical concepts can also be reinforced by employing materials—*e.g.*, weight (scale), temperature (thermometer), linear measurement (ruler), properties of a circle (compass and protractor). In more advanced mathematics, an algebraic equation can be "seen" when plotted upon the X and Y axes of a coordinate graph.

Other areas also lend themselves to concretization: maps, charts, graphs in geography, a "time line" for history, various apparatus and equipment for science, audiovisual aids for language arts and other subject areas.

There are several reasons for making these materials a part of the educational experiences for those children presenting difficulty in abstract thinking:

(1) The most obvious advantage is that the materials are experienced sensorially, hence they are more "real" (meaningful) to these children than is a pure idea or symbol.

(2) These materials offer multisensory experiences rather

than rely on one sense modality. Such experiences are often recommended for these children (Strauss and Lehtinen 1947: 127-90; Rhodes 1966: 407; Epps *et al.* 1958). Particularly important is the opportunity these materials provide for the children to touch and manipulate. Many of these children seem to need this intersensory feedback (*i.e.,* the tactile corroboration of visual sensory data) to help them interpret their environment more reliably. Other examples of multisensory activities are the use of sandpaper cutouts of numbers and letters (which allow the child to feel what he sees), the Fernald method of teaching spelling (combining the kinesthetic sense with the auditory sense—the child "writes" the word in the air as he says the letters) and teaching counting by letting the child see a number of objects, count them tactually without looking at them, and count them by "listening to them" (*e.g.,* the teacher instructs the child to look away and to guess how many blocks there are by listening to each strike the table as the teacher places them there).

(3) The use of these materials can serve to make the lesson more interesting; this factor of interest is pertinent to the problem areas of attention span as well as of motivation.

It is important that the teacher use these materials discriminately. He must know which materials to use and why they are recommended. He must know when to use them and how to use them. The lesson's effectiveness is sure to be increased by a careful consideration of such routines as: When is the best time to distribute the materials? How shall I distribute them?—*i.e.,* Can I let the children choose their materials as they are being distributed or shall I make the choice for them? Should I distribute the materials, let a student distribute them or instruct the children to "take one and pass the rest back"? Should I let the materials remain on the children's desks all period or collect them when not in use, thereby diminishing clutter and distractibility? How shall materials be collected? Should they be stored in the children's desks or elsewhere? How can I discourage misuse of materials?

UTILIZE CONCEPTUALIZATION ACTIVITIES. Just as there are activities, basically perceptual in nature, designed to help perceptually impaired children, there are conceptualization experiences that aim at improving children's ability to conceptualize. Sorting activities come close to the heart of abstracting, for in sorting (object, pictures, words, etc.) we conscientiously seek similarities while ignoring trivial differences; in fact, the ability to sort or to categorize denotes the ability to make generalizations. The ability to classify (*i.e.*, to group) enables us to systematize large areas of the outside world which would otherwise remain chaotic (Strauss and Kephart 1955: 114). Humphrey (1944: 50) further points out the importance of these means of structuring the elements of our external world:

> Like every other living organism, the human being may be envisaged as struggling . . . to preserve an identity of organic pattern in a chaotic world. In order that this process of self-preservation may be advantageously effected, the organism must be such that it discerns, in a measure gradually increasing as evolution advances, similarities existent under the superficial variation in its environment. Only by such discernment of similarities can the organism survive; without it organic response must be chaotic in a chaotic-seeming world. The ability to discern similarities hidden beneath divergence is the ability to generalize. . . . Such ability has reached its climax in the human species.

Inasmuch as concept formation involves the consideration of present perceptions against a background of elements that are retained from similar experiences in the past (Strauss and Kephart 1955: 115), memory is a component of abstract thinking and conceptualization. As such, memory-promoting activities are needed in the curriculum of children whose conceptualization abilities are impaired.

Similarly, language experiences are also necessary. This is so because language (*i.e.*, words or symbols) enable us to demarcate and hold together conceptual similarities and conceptual relationships that have been observed. Language, in its broad sense, includes not only vocabulary but relationships, understanding of shades of differences, and ability to listen, as well.

Siegel (1961: 117–21) suggests some specific conceptualization experiences:*

[1.] *Opposites*
Use sentences which contain contrasts. Let the child try to supply the last word. For example:
"Summers are hot, but winters are ———."
"My friend was dirty, but I was ———."
"One shoe is wet, but the other is ———."
Use two small dolls, two puppets or two pictures of people. Tell the child that these two people are very different. Mention one fact about your "person" (this fact can be real or imaginary). For example, say, "My man is clean." Encourage the child to tell the opposite about his. Sometimes the child can understand the meaning of opposite if you tell him that his "person" is different. Another way is to use the word "but" as a contrast, and let him complete the last word of a sentence ("My man is tall, but yours is ———."

[2.] *Memory box*
Put three to five common objects in a cigar box. (These objects may include a key, coin, comb, pencil, nail, cube of sugar, etc.) Show them to the child and discuss them with him. Cover his eyes and remove one of the objects. Let him look at the remaining objects and try to guess which has been taken. The number of objects may be increased gradually.

This can also be done by sense of touch (tactile). Instead of letting him look at the remaining objects, he must feel them and try to determine the missing one.

[3.] *Sorting pictures by category*
Collect pictures, from old magazines, depicting broad categories such as rides, drinks, animals, furniture, etc. Use five to ten

---

* Reprinted with permission from *Helping the Brain Injured Child*, New York Association for Brain Injured Children, 1961.

pictures for each category. Mount each picture on a 7″ × 7″ piece of cardboard. The child's task is to sort them by category.

At first, place one picture from each category in front of him. Discuss them with him. "Where will we put the rides? the animals?" etc. Give him one picture at a time. Gradually, let him work from the entire collection. Large envelopes may be used for each group of pictures.

[4.] *Magic pegs (categories)*

Divide a piece of 3″ × 20″ wood into ten 3″ × 2″ sections. Paint each section a different color. You may use only two or three colors, but no two adjoining sections should be the same color. Drill three holes vertically in the center of each section. The holes should be spaced at least ¾″ apart.

Pretend that the "magic" three pegs belong to one category, say, animals. If the child names one animal, he places a peg in a hole in the first section. If he names the second, he places a peg in the second hole of that section, etc. When he finishes this first section, the magic pegs belong to a different category. In this manner, proceed from section to section in a left-right direction.

[5.] *Arranging in chronological order*

Collect or draw pictures illustrating four chronological stages (*e.g.*, an infant, a small child, an adult, an old man). Mount these on 4″ × 4″ cards. Mix them up. The child must arrange them in chronological order, from left to right. Emphasize concepts of "first," "next," "last," etc.

Other examples illustrating chronological order might be stages in the growth of a plant or a tree, or pictures from a familiar story, which are to be arranged sequentially.

[6.] *Riddles*

Ask the child riddles about a variety of subjects—animals, rides, people, etc. Give him more and more clues, until he guesses the answer. Let him try to make up riddles for you to guess.

[7.] *Recognizing absurdities*

Tell the child a brief story which contains an absurdity. See if he can tell what is wrong. Some examples of absurdities are: eating supper in the morning; wearing a raincoat on a sunny day; buying bread in a hardware store; etc.

Show him a picture that has missing parts, objects placed

upside down, or with some other element incorrect. See if he can tell what is wrong.

[8.] *"Which is different?"*

Using the geometric forms from previous activities, place four of them in front of the child. Of the four, three will be the same, and one will be different (*e.g.*, three squares and one circle). Let him tell which one is different. Let him try it blindfolded, by feeling the pieces. Vary this activity by using more concrete objects—silverware, different colored crayons, various sized buttons, etc.

[9.] *Strengthening concepts (prepositions)*

Use a rubber band and a small match box. Direct the child to put the rubber band in the box, on the box, under the box, near the box, around the box, far from the box. This can be done with various materials: penny-bank, ball-box, etc.

Some of the above suggestions which seem particularly suitable for young children can be augmented by more mature activities for older children. Words (instead of pictures) can be sorted. Poetry, drama and the game of Concentration can promote memory. Language experiences can be provided for by certain party games such as Twenty Questions, What's My Line?, charades, etc. The area of clerical practice (filing, alphabetizing, indexing, etc.) is full of opportunities to classify and arrange.

In addition to the above activities, a consideration of modes of behavior that characterize an abstract attitude (Goldstein and Sheerer 1941: 1–8) will suggest organized classroom activities. For example, a sequentialized approach to jokes and cartoons (*i.e.*, easier ones followed by more complex ones) can help children learn to grasp the essential of a given whole; analogies, metaphors and finding the common denominator can promote the ability to abstract common properties reflectively; encouraging children to give verbal accounts of projected motor activities (*e.g.*, to draw a map and describe the path along which one walks daily or to describe sequentially the movements involved in swimming) assists their learning to plan ahead ideationally and to account verbally for acts to themselves and to others.

BE AWARE OF SPECIAL LEARNING PRINCIPLES. Kirk (1962: 120–1) lists principles for the education of the mentally retarded child. Since the brain-injured and the emotionally disturbed also frequently present problems in abstract thinking, these principles would seem equally applicable to them. In fact, Kirk terms these principles as "the best practices in learning":

1. Progress is from the known to the unknown, using concrete material to foster understanding of more abstract facts.
2. The child is helped to transfer known abilities from one situation to another, rather than being expected to make generalizations spontaneously.
3. The teacher uses many repetitions in a variety of experiences.
4. Learning is stimulated through exciting situations.
5. Inhibitions are avoided by presenting one idea at a time and presenting learning situations by sequential steps.
6. Learning is reinforced through using a variety of sense modalities—visual, oral, auditory, kinesthetic.

Even these principles should be regarded as approaches and guidelines; it must remain within the province of the classroom teacher to decide when (and if) they pertain to the case at hand. For example, to attempt to inject excitement into the classroom experiences of a hyperactive, impulsive, excitable brain-injured child might prove chaotic; yet who can deny that this child, too, must be interested and motivated in order to learn? Similarly, brain-injured children and emotionally disturbed children who do not present learning problems do not require excessive repetition, but may need modifications of a different kind.

Behavioral Problems

The term "behavior," in a broad sense, encompasses man's total repertoire of interaction with his environment. It includes covert as well as overt reaction to stimuli. Instinct, habit, personality traits and life functions (*e.g.*, the "behavior" of one's digestive organs) as well as the act of learning (cognitive styles and strategies, preferred sensory mode, etc.) can be subsumed under it.

Kirk (1962: 330) defines a behavior deviation as "that behavior of a child which (1) has a detrimental effect on his development and adjustment and/or (2) interferes with the lives of other people." Kirk's second criterion parallels the dictionary definition (Webster 1956: 162) of "behavior," which stresses behavior toward others: "Manner of behaving, whether good or bad; conduct; manners; carriage of oneself with respect to propriety of morals; deportment. It expresses external appearance or action. . . . Behavior is the manner of our behaving ourselves toward others. . . ." This specific aspect of behavior will be stressed here since, for sheer survival purposes, the classroom teacher must immediately deal with the child who misbehaves toward others. Indeed, if the problem is grave enough—that is, sufficiently noisy, disruptive or dangerous—he cannot defer coping, even for a moment, as he might do in the case of a withdrawn child, a child with tics or a child with limited cognitive skill.

It is well known that the children in question frequently present behavior problems in the classroom: The slow learner may misbehave in his bid for attention or perhaps because of difficulty in understanding what is expected of him; the brain-injured child's impulsivity and low frustration level are often at the root of his classroom misbehavior; the overt behavior of emotionally disturbed children as well as the actions of socially maladjusted children who "regularly disregard broader social values and rules as a matter of course, substituting in their stead the values and rules of their peer group [Pate 1963: 340]" usually result in classroom behavior problems.

The behavior problems encountered in the regular classroom may be of such magnitude that a special class placement is warranted; however, it is equally possible for a mildly handicapped child enrolled in a regular classroom to present significant but "copable" behavior problems. The following are some suggestions by which the regular classroom teacher might help the mildly handicapped child maintain favorable behavior:

ESTABLISH ROUTINES. Lack of structure in classroom routines often increases tension and anxiety in children, especially those presenting learning and/or behavior problems. Kirk (1962: 336) states that "behavior problems are the outcome of frustration resulting from the discrepancy between the child's capacity to behave and the requirement of the environment." To the extent that unroutinized classroom procedures (distribution of materials, entering and dismissals, storage of individual pupil's books and outer clothing, assignment of homework, the use of the pupil to give oral messages to his parents, etc.,) require more of the child, these can be seen as anxiety-producing.

In discussing the education of the young brain-injured child in the school (and at home) Siegel (1961: 52-3) points out the importance of establishing routines:*

> Any classroom teacher knows that the first few days (and often more) are devoted to the establishing of routines. Considerable time, effort, and energy are spent in assigning seats to the children, showing them how, when and where to hang their coats in the closet, and how to enter and leave the classroom. They learn the correct aisle in which to stand, the specific exit to use in dismissal, and the proper way to ask permission to speak. Rules are set up for the distribution and care of materials, the passing

* Reprinted with permission from *Helping the Brain Injured Child*, New York Association for Brain Injured Children, 1961.

of papers to the teacher, and for the collection of milk and cookie money. Indeed, the younger children are taught how and even when to drink water and to use the bathroom.

Why such an emphasis on routines? There are several reasons. Basically, classroom routines are the foundation upon which all other learning experience can be built—a prerequisite of a sort, for living together. An individual, not in the company of others, would hardly have need to routinize his behavior. If he called out, it could distract no one. If he changed seats, it would inconvenience no one. If he used the "wrong" exit, it would interfere with no one. In the classroom, however, the need for routine becomes obvious.

Picture the chaos that would be created by Row 3 standing in the aisle to the right and Row 4 using the one to the left. Not only do routines increase the efficiency and the safety of the classroom, but they foster the social growth of the individual. He learns to be considerate of others: he does not take their seats; he does not call out when they are talking. He learns to exercise self-control: he is thirsty but he doesn't run to get a drink of water; he wants to play ball now, but he must wait for his gym period later. Finally, routines become habit. The effort, thought and energy spent in the performance of these routine activities, when they were not automatic, can now be devoted to other accomplishments.

Routines are especially important for the brain-injured child. When he meets with success in activities such as eating, washing, dressing, and caring for belongings, he becomes more acceptable to his family, particularly his parents. Indeed, he grows more acceptable to himself. He has succeeded in organizing part of his environment. Chaos is replaced with order.

Then, too, the sheer mastery of these routines constitutes an accomplishment—a success—a feeling of achievement which comes neither often nor easily to the brain-injured child. In a sense, this feeling of success—this ability to become more organized—is basic to his existence.

Another factor is the element of transfer which is implied in the establishment of these basic routines. The act of routinizing involves self-control, inhibition, and the capacity to conform. If the brain-injured child can learn and obey the "rules" for eating, dressing, etc., might he not also use this capacity for self-control in learning "rules" of conduct, manners, and the give-and-take of social intercourse?

Not only is the overall ability to adapt to routines necessary; the activities themselves are equally significant. Eating habits, table manners, speed and accuracy in dressing, cleanliness, care and orderly arrangements of belongings—these are all important for present and future social activities. Certainly, the establishment of these basic habits enhances the possibilities of success in later experiences in school, day camps, training centers, and other such programs.

Don't Let Situations Snowball. Many unpleasant classroom situations can be prevented if they are stopped at the very beginning. This requires an alert attitude on the part of the teacher—a certain flexibility, if you will—a mental set that permits the teacher, while fully engrossed in the act of teaching, to scan continually the class, both auditorially and visually, for any initial signs of situational behavior problems: hitting or kicking, shouting, name calling, destroying property, creating excessive noise, etc. Clearly, such actions have a beginning and, if permitted to continue, can increase in intensity and complexity. Some suggestions (Redl and Wineman 1957: 402–9) for preventing the mushrooming of these situations follow:

(1) Use of "signal interference." By this technique, the teacher signals (a gesture, a glance in the child's direction, a brief verbal comment, a sudden cessation of activities, etc.) to a child who is beginning to misbehave that what he is doing is unacceptable. In the early stages of misbehavior, the child is more capable of maintaining self-control; thus, this initial signal may prevent an "anger feeding anger" situation in which negativism, hostility and possible aggression become mobilized to a "point of no return" level (Blackham 1967: 144–50).

(2) Use of proximity control. Sometimes, standing near an

excited child, perhaps touching him lightly, has a calming effect. Not only does this proximity communicate to the child that the teacher is "close to me, hence he likes me," but it also serves to distract him from the stimuli (people or things) which originally engaged his attention and have threatened to ignite undesirable behavior.

BE CONSISTENT. Children who evidence learning and/or behavior disorders often benefit by a consistent approach on the part of the teacher. Consistency offers structure to the brain-injured, clarity to the mentally retarded and sets limits for the emotionally disturbed. Many classroom routines and procedures lend themselves to a policy of consistency. For example, there is a rule in most classrooms that children must raise their hands in order to get the teacher's permission to speak. Generally, classroom teachers try to abide by that rule; however, very often, in the teacher's enthusiasm during a discussion lesson, he may actually (albeit unknowingly) invite a child to call out (*i.e.*, the teacher asks a question in such a manner as to show that he expects the child to call out; the child calls out the answer; the teacher praises his correct response, thereby reinforcing his behavior). However, a few moments later, another child calls out and is reprimanded for it. Now, it has been observed that the children who are most frequently reprimanded are the mildly retarded or brain-injured; it may be that they are less capable than their nonhandicapped classmates of evaluating the teacher's mood and judging when he will permit a relaxing of the standards. Surely, such a double standard can prove injurious to children who already have poor self-concepts, and may result in negative behavior.

The teacher should strive for consistency: Either the children must *always* raise their hands before speaking (in which case the teacher will have to do a lot of observing, reminding, praising, etc.) or they should *never* be asked to do so (some mature secondary classes can function in this manner). Another possibility is *planned inconsistency:* the children generally must adhere to the rule, but in certain specific instances (clubs, home room period, group guidance, leadership training, etc.) the rule can be waived.

INVESTIGATE SITUATIONS. Very often, teachers, in their zeal to show that certain behavior is not acceptable will punish the victim as well as the perpetrator. For example, aren't fights often broken up with the teacher's "I don't care who started it"? It may very well be that a mildly handicapped child in the regular classroom is perceived as "different" by his normal peers, is discriminated against and is actually physically assaulted by one of his classmates; it behooves the teacher to consider that possibility and not automatically assign equal guilt to the two participants. Without suggesting that the classroom teacher assume the role of an inquisitor, it might still be appropriate for him to examine and inquire to some extent. Certainly, the handicapped child should not be punished by the teacher for having been punished by his classmates.

PLANNED IGNORING. At times, the teacher's attempt to interfere with a child's unacceptable behavior calls attention to it and can serve to kindle rather than extinguish it. In fact, some children may act out only because they want to witness the effect of their performance on the teacher. Planned ignoring of these outbursts denies the child any reinforcement of his misconduct, and he is unlikely to repeat it. Needless to say, it requires considerable teacher skill and insight to determine which acts to ignore and which require interference. Basically, interference should be limited only to those acts which "carry too heavy an intensity charge within themselves or which would not stop from their own exhaustion unless directly interfered with" (Redl and Wineman 1957: 400–1).

DEVELOP AN APPROPRIATE COMMUNICATION PATTERN. The teacher's communication pattern is important. It is essential that the teacher speak slowly, not too loudly and not too much: Loud and rapid speech can in itself be too exciting, particularly to emotionally disturbed and brain-injured children; the slow learner may experience difficulty listening to and understanding large doses of verbalisms; the brain-injured child, who often has auditory perception problems, may require more listening time; the culturally deprived child may be inexperienced in dealing with large quantities of adult speech (Riessman 1962: 82).

A tempo change (slow to a little more rapid speech, soft to somewhat louder speech, listening activities to doing activities, etc.) is often helpful. Such changes can be beneficial in preventing behavior problems and rendering the lesson more interesting.

Barsch (1965: 339) adds the following suggestions: limiting the language of directives to the bare essentials, reducing them virtually to "telegraphic speech," avoiding ambiguous words, accompanying words with gestures, maintaining visual contact with the listener, avoiding speaking while the child is in the midst of work and even touching the child to signal that verbal directions are about to begin.

USE THE CHILD'S WEAKNESS TO ADVANTAGE. At times a child's weakness can be used to advantage. For example, a distractible child can frequently, and easily, be "distracted" out of his negative mood or away from background interests to the foreground task at hand. This sudden change of subject or redirection of activity has been called "restructuring" (Redl and Wineman 1957: 426–29) and is appropriate for groups of children as well as for individuals. Blackham (1967: 148–49) points out that motor outlets (performing an errand, walking outside to get a drink, etc.) are sometimes required by emotionally disturbed children who cannot readily concentrate during quiet activities for long periods of time. Similarly, perserveration implies a capacity for "drive" and inability to shift easily from one situation to another; the classroom teacher can, at times, assign such a child to tasks that require no shifting and into which his "drive" can be properly channeled. There is, of course, a semantic problem here. The child would now be *persevering*—that is, working purposefully, rather than perseverating (responding to a stimulus long after the need for such response has gone), but it seems likely that, in both cases, it is his basic inability to shift that is operating.

TRAIN SPECIFICALLY FOR INDEPENDENT WORK. One of the prime concerns of those who decide whether or not to place a mildly handicapped child in a regular classroom is the child's ability to work independently. Special classes, being reduced in size, enable the teacher to devote more time to the individual; indeed, some placements such as home instruction, some hospital classes and various tutorial programs offer a one-to-one relationship.

In the regular classroom, however, the teacher may complain, and justifiably so, "I know that he can do the work, but he can't do a thing unless I am right there with him." Now, there is a direct relationship between inability to work independently and classroom behavior problems: Namely, children who are supposed to be working independently but who are unable to do so often engage in misconduct. The teacher might ameliorate this condition by specifically teaching the child to work independently. Whatever the reason for this dependency (an emotionally disturbed child may need the teacher's proximity for psychological reasons; a brain-injured child may be too impulsive and distractible to work alone; the slow learner may not understand the task) the teacher should clearly separate the task of learning new subject matter and the task of working independently. It is probably too much for the child who cannot work independently to do both at the same time.

The child can possibly gain in his ability to work unaided if:

(1) The initial tasks are familiar to him and are entirely within his repertoire (the so-called "success-assured" activities).

(2) The initial tasks are repetitive, well-defined and preferably manipulative in nature (sorting, matching, assembling, etc.).

(3) The tasks are gradually increased in time, level and complexity.

(4) The child's growth toward independency is reinforced (praise, special tokens of merit, etc.).

EMPLOY A GOOD MENTAL HYGIENE APPROACH. Children often misbehave because they are rejected and are led to reject themselves. Clearly, any approach that bolsters the child's self-concept can go a long way toward improving classroom conduct. (Such an approach is very much in order for the withdrawn as well as for the acting-out child.) Use of success-assured activities, assignment to tasks requiring responsibilities (monitor, etc.), use of praise, avoidance of negative value judgments and direct appeal to other members of the class have already been mentioned.

Sometimes, getting a child to take pride in his appearance is an effective technique. Correct attire, suitable posture and attention to personal hygiene can render the child more acceptable to others and to himself as well. Obviously, this is a very personal matter and should be handled individually, in private or subtly via hygiene or biology lessons or in well-chosen units of work.

Another helpful device is to try to "tune-in" on the child's mental set which led him to the wrong answer. The teacher, by letting the child know that he understands what he was thinking, diminishes the "wrongness" of the answer and at the same time communicates to the child his understanding.

Redl and Wineman (1957: 412–23) suggest (1) tension decontamination through humor—that is, "kidding" the child out of his misbehavior, (2) hurdle help—giving the child additional help at specific times (that is, when he encounters a specifically frustrating obstacle related to some well-defined goal, which, if faced unaided, may evoke overt negative behavior and reduce self-esteem) and (3) using interpretation as interference—that is, explaining or interpreting the rule (or situation) in such a way that it is acceptable—or at least understandable—to the child, thereby interfering with any possible buildup to acting-out behavior and ensuing guilt feelings.

USE OF DIRECT APPEAL TO CHILD. Often, instead of looking for drastic means of interfering with negative behavior (prohibition, punishing, etc.) a direct appeal to the child can be effective (Redl and Wineman 1957: 429–33). Such appeals as "It's quite warm indoors today, and the sooner you stop talking, the quicker we can get outside in the shade" and "I know Jack isn't as good a ball player as you, but if you hit him every time he makes an error, he'll get nervous and won't do any better. Let's try to be friendly to him and encourage him and maybe he'll improve" can be helpful.

FULL PREPARATION OF LESSON. This, perhaps, is the crucial key to maintaining favorable classroom behavior. It is obvious that a child cannot conform and misbehave at the same time; hence, if the lesson is planned in such a way as to foster conformity, the chances for outbursts of negative behavior will be drastically diminished. By carefully considering the aim and scope of the lesson, by judicious selection and preparation of materials and activities, by employing skill in planning the lesson's development (the order of activities) and by deliberate inclusion of tempo changes, changes of activity, opportunity to *do* as well as to discuss, etc., the teacher will be setting the stage for favorable classroom behavior.

This is one of the greatest paradoxes in teaching: "How can I teach a child—that is, get him to work—when I can't even get him to behave?" Yet, once the child *is* working, he is no longer misbehaving.

Social Immaturity

Children who suffer from learning and/or behavior problems are often socially immature as well. This is probably a result of (1) their specific intellectual or emotional deficit (*e.g.*, a slow learner might not readily grasp the rules of give-and-take of social intercourse; an emotionally disturbed child may be too anxious and preoccupied with himself to perform adequately in social situations) and (2) social rejection by their peers. In a classic sociogram study (Bower 1962: 627), in which a class play served as the projective instrument, it was found that normal children in regular classes tended to choose emotionally disturbed children for hostile, negative and inadequate roles and, conversely, omitted them from positive roles. Similarly, the mentally retarded child in the regular classroom is often seen to have a lower social status than his nonhandicapped classmates (Baldwin 1958: 106–8).

Parents of these children, as well as professionals who work with them, frequently feel that their social immaturity constitutes a far graver problem than their shortcomings in academic skills (Siegel 1967: 356–57). After all, how often is a child asked to multiply $7\frac{1}{2} \times 4$? But he does come face to face with his peers daily, whether in planned activity or in spontaneous informal situations.

The process of socializing is a highly complicated one. We generally lose sight of this when observing normal children because their social interactions proceed so smoothly. However, observe a child with a mild learning or behavioral deficit as he mingles with nonhandicapped children, and the complexities of social intercourse become painfully clear. How does one learn when to listen and when to talk? How does one know when to talk about himself and when to talk about others? When is it appropriate to change the subject? Must there be a steady flow of conversation or is group silence ever in order? When should a topic be conversed "to the hilt" and when should it receive only cursory verbal attention?

It is probably much more difficult to teach socialization skills than it is to teach a specific subject area; there are, however, some ways in which the regular classroom teacher can help mildly handicapped children to improve socially.

PROVIDE EXPERIENCES FOR SOCIALIZATION. Undoubtedly, one

factor militating against the social maturity of mildly handicapped children is their lack of social experiences. Normal children—engaging in formal as well as informal social situations daily, accepted by their peers, possessing adequate "feedback" mechanism (by which they can reliably interpret the effect of their actions on the group)—grow continually. The mildly handicapped child, perhaps because of parental overprotection, but certainly because of peer rejection, is denied this necessary experience; hence, the social gap between him and his nonhandicapped counterpart is widened.

There are many situations within the school for providing opportunities for socialization: the unit method of work, any joint project (class mural, preparation for trip or party, community project such as neighborhood cleanliness drive, etc.), the "buddy" system of studying (*e.g.,* for a spelling test), sending two or three children on a common errand, trips, party games, group athletics and so on.

GIVE SPECIFIC INSTRUCTIONS IN SOCIAL SKILLS. Often a mildly handicapped child may encounter difficulty in incidental learning. This might be related to (1) the brain-injured child's faulty feedback mechanism (Strauss and Kephart 1955: 2f–10f) and (2) the slow learner's relative difficulty in transferring what he has learned in one specific situation to similar situations (Kirk 1962: 121). At any rate, it is safe to say that, in some cases, mildly handicapped children should be specifically taught the things that many normal children can grasp incidentally. (The nonhandicapped child in the regular classroom can also benefit from this specific instruction since it can serve to *reinforce* his incidental learning.)

Rules of etiquette can be taught and practiced at all levels. A home economic class can include in its curriculum table manners as well as correct "hostessing" skills. Grooming and personal hygiene can be taught in hygiene and biology classes. Telephone etiquette can be considered at elementary levels as well as in the secondary clerical practices program. There are many classroom situations that entail audience deportment (listening to a classmate read aloud or recite, listening to committee reports or to a guest speaker, attending auditorium programs, etc.). A class newspaper can have a question-and-answer column devoted to etiquette. Classroom discussion—particularly in group guidance classes—can be devoted to the topic of appropriate (and inappropriate) social behavior. There are readily available materials (films, stories, plays, etc.) which can assist the classroom teacher in his endeavors to impart social skills to his pupils. Games can be particularly useful in that (1) they usually have a common goal, thereby promoting socialization and group sharing, and (2) they often require that the participants practice certain basic elements of etiquette (*e.g.*, the prerequisite asking of "May I?" in Giant Steps, taking turns at bat in baseball, etc.).

IMPROVE SELF-CONCEPT. A child suffering from learning and/or behavior problems can very likely develop anxiety and a poor self-concept. This, in turn, can render him less effective socially: An anxious, unsure child may try too hard in a group situation and what he says may not ring true; a child who feels inferior to his peers may then act (behave) at an inferior level—that is, feelings of inadequacy can lead a child to defenses, façades and subterfuges (Freidus n.d.: 17; Blackham 1967: 154; Krupp and Schwartzberg 1960) such as an inappropriate smile, contrariness, gullibility or clownish behavior. Gardner (1968: 486) points out that a minimally brain-injured child may develop a clowning, even a "freakish" reaction, employing the rationale of "Hey. Look at me. See how I'm behaving? I'm really just kidding around. I don't have to act this way. I can 'turn it on' at will." The argument, though, is a specious one, since, as Gardner explains, the child cannot "turn it off" at will.

Plainly, any of the suggestions already mentioned in which the classroom teacher can help the child improve his self-concept (use of success-assured activities, use of praise, improving the image which the child presents to his classmates, etc.) and reduce anxiety (small doses, nominal use of time-limited experiences, a selection of activities in which there are no "wrong" answers, use of humor, etc.) can facilitate the emergence of social maturity.

TRAIN IN COMMUNICATION. Social maturity is very much related to skill in communicating. In fact, the two can be viewed as almost synonymous since the chief way in which one demonstrates his social maturity (or lack of it) is through spontaneous conversation. Slow learners, particularly those enrolling in school for the first time, usually show a disproportionately large number of speech defects, inadequate grammatical skills and poor ability to express themselves clearly (Johnson 1963: 196). The brain-injured child, even the minimally handicapped, may present some language problem reflecting a basic difficulty in conceptualization; in addition, there may be other factors which militate against his effective communication skills. These are (1) perseveration—a tendency to repeat a subject or "talk a subject to death", (2) impulsivity—lack of self-control when silence is appropriate, (3) "feedback" difficulty—inability to determine readily the effect of his conversational contributions upon others, (4) egocentricity—too much talking about "me", (5) distractibility—talking about irrelevant subjects and (6) minor speech problems related to articulatory defects or faulty auditory perception.

There are also some psychological factors which can have an adverse effect upon a child's ability to communicate. Emotionally disturbed children (as well as slow learners and mildly brain-injured children) may be anxiety-ridden, this extreme tension and concern diminishing the likelihood of effective communication; similarly, inappropriate defense mechanisms can take the form of inappropriate communication (out-of-place laughter, acting and talking like an "oddball," taking an unusual and untenable position but holding onto it, etc.).

An unfortunate cycle emerges. These children may speak

incorrectly only part of the time. However, those who come in contact with them (children as well as adults, laymen as well as professionals, even family members) may develop a mental set which makes them "tune out" (*i.e.*, frown, interrupt or, in general, show an inability if not an unwillingness to listen to) *all* of their utterances, even the appropriate ones.

It is important, then, that the classroom teacher devote some part of the curriculum to facilitating language development. Activities which stress listening, auditory discrimination, auditory memory, various language concepts and correct articulation are recommended. Siegel (1961: 115, 126–8) has described some of these activities:*

1. *Discriminating sounds*

Blindfold the child. Make various sounds—jingle keys, crumple paper, turn on the water faucet, strike a piano key, rap on the table, open a zipper, etc.—and see if he can identify these sounds. Clap your hands either loudly or softly, and see if he can tell you which sounds are loud and which are soft. Tip-toe to various sections of the room; call out to him, clap your hands, or make some other pre-arranged sound; see if he can locate the source of the sound.

2. *Imitate rhythmic patterns*

Clap your hands in specific rhythmic pattern, using various combinations of long and short "notes." Play various rhythms on a drum. Use very simple rhythms. Let the child try to imitate. If he misses, discuss the pattern. Play it for him again. Drawing a picture of the pattern, using dots and dashes, will sometimes help him to "see" the rhythm (– – –.–), (...–), (– –...–), etc. Let him try again.

3. *Melody recognition*

Play familiar songs on the piano, or hum them to the child. Can he identify the song? Play only a portion of the song, perhaps only three or four notes. Let him try to name the tune. If he can't, play it again, adding a note each time. . . .

* Reprinted with permission from *Helping the Brain Injured Child,* New York Association for Brain Injured Children, 1961.

4. *From words to sentences*
Say a word and encourage the child to tell you something about it. For variation, show him a picture and ask him to tell something about it.

5. *Sentence completion*
Recite a sentence, omitting the last word. Let the child try to complete it. The sentence can be related to a story with which he is familiar, or to an actual occurrence. Some examples are:
   a. "Tomorrow we will go to John's ———."
   b. "Father will come home from ———."
   c. "Little Red Riding Hood met the ———."
If necessary, cue the child, by making the sound of the initial consonant.

6. *Riddles using initial consonants*
Ask the child a question providing him with the initial consonant sound.
"I am thinking of a big animal that begins with zzz . . ."
"I am thinking of something that shines at night, and it sounds like mmmm...."

7. *Imitating sounds*
Ask the child to make sounds of various animals:

cat: meow   dog: woof-woof
duck: quack-quack cow: Moo
bird: tweet   sheep: baa-baa

Then reverse the process. Make the sound and ask him to name the animal.

8. *Counting syllables*
Teach syllables by exaggerating the separate sounds of one, two or three-syllable words. Speak slowly, clapping your hands on each syllable. Let the child do the same. Make sets of pictures illustrating one, two and three-syllable nouns. Let the child sort the pictures according to the number of syllables each noun contains.

9. *Syllable cards*
A child may mispronounce words having two, three or more syllables. He is probably confused by the many parts of the word, and may be reversing some of the sounds.

Print the word on a strip of cardboard. Cut this strip into syllables. Let him see and pronounce each separately; then join them. Sometimes, it helps to make each letter out of sandpaper, and let him feel the various parts of the word.

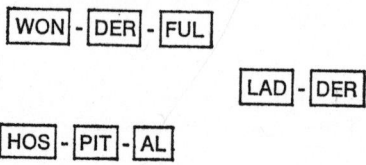

10. *Articulation activities*

Blowing is a good exercise for strengthening breath control and lip movements. Blow soap bubbles, blow a ping-pong ball for distance and accuracy. Blow a paper boat across a tub of water. The latter two can be game situations.

Tongue exercise, too, is often needed. Let the child imitate the movements of your tongue. Stretch it all the way out, point it upwards, bend it to either side, touch the roof of your mouth with it, rub it across your teeth, etc.

A variation would be to place a lollypop near the child's mouth (touching his face) and let him try to lick it. He must do this with his tongue only, and is not allowed to move his head. Vary the position of the lollypop, and increase the distance from the child's mouth gradually.

11. *Quotation Content Discrimination* (Siegel, Gisonti and Posnack 1966). Children must listen critically to direct quotations such as "Good morning, Mrs. Brown," "May I please get a drink of water?", "Vincent, will you erase the blackboard?", etc. and judge which of two possible characters (in this case, the teacher or the pupil) is the speaker. For variation, other sets of characters can be used (*e.g.,* doctor and patient, father and son, salesman and customer, etc.). This can be a class game; more mature students can be encouraged to make up their own quotations.

12. *Visualization—language activities.* The dual ability (1) visualization (*i.e.*, imagining, remembering or thinking about scenes and objects rather than actually seeing them) and (2) translating such visualizations into verbal language is an important developmental aspect of communication. Some of the visualization-language activities suggested by Getman (1962: 95, 99–100) can be adapted for classroom use.

(a) Describe any object or the clothes and appearance of a pupil and the child tries to name the object or the pupil from the teacher's description.

(b) Ask a child to describe a trip he has just taken or to describe the path from his house to the school.

(c) Have a child close his eyes and tell where various objects in the classroom are located.

(d) Instruct the child to try to recall the day's occurrences and to list them in chronological order.

Other activities such as games, drama, music, reporting of various kinds, auditory discrimination training in phonics, reading comprehension skills, can all serve in fostering the development of communication skills.

Since how one communicates is a highly personal consideration, the teacher must be sensitive to the emotional needs of the pupil. For example, a child may have to be prodded out of his egocentric pattern of thinking and talking; he must be encouraged to listen to others and to focus his energies (attention, thought, verbalisms) on the appropriate topic or person rather than on himself. Such prodding, however, must be gentle rather than violent, matter-of-fact rather than condemning and should be unobtrusive—between the teacher and the particular child, rather than a matter for the entire class.

DEVELOP SOCIAL-RECREATIONAL SKILLS. Observers have often noted that the child with a mild learning or behavior problem is at his best (*i.e.*, most like the normal child) when engaged in a physical task or activity alongside normal children similarly engaged. That is to say, if a slow learner and a group of normal children are swimming together—and swimming equally well—then, at that moment, the slow learner is as normal as the other participants. Seen in this light, the school gymnasium program or "club" period, by offering activities such as swimming, bowling, table tennis, folk dancing and social dancing, bridge, checkers and chess, perhaps even skating and bicycling, can be instrumental in nurturing the social maturity of the mildly handicapped child.

USE A SEQUENTIAL APPROACH. Any efforts to assist socially immature children are almost certainly doomed to failure if sequence is overlooked. The following sequential points should be considered by the classroom teacher in structuring socialization experiences for these children.

1. Students of early childhood development know that peripheral play precedes parallel play which, in turn, precedes group play. Similarly, a mildly handicapped child in the regular classroom may need lots of experience socializing with one child before being ready for group socialization. The teacher can encourage such a one-to-one relationship by judicious seating and grouping, sending the two children on joint errands, committee assignments during units of work, the "buddy" system, etc.

2. Group socialization experiences for the socially immature child should be carefully graded in time dosages, degree of complexity of the activity and degree of teacher supervision.

3. Many socially immature children relate to younger children with more facility than they do to children of their own ages. The teacher can "match" a socially immature older child with a younger classmate in many classroom situations; in some instances, he can assign this child during free periods to groups of younger children for whom the older child serves as a "helper" (or tutor), reading to them, acting as safety monitor during a brief trip, playing ball with them as their team captain, etc. (Not only do these activities provide meaningful socialization experiences to this child, but the obvious "pres-

tige" factor can strengthen his self-concept). Gradually he can be encouraged and guided in spending more time with children of his own age.

REFERENCES

Baldwin, Willie Kate, "The Educable Mentally Retarded Child in the Regular Classroom." *Exceptional Children,* 25: 106–108, 112 (November, 1958).

Barsch, Ray H., "Six Factors in Learning," in Jerome Hellmuth, ed., *Learning Disorders,* Vol. 1. Seattle, Wash., Special Child Publications, Seattle Sequin School, 1965, pp. 329–43.

Beck, Harry S., "Detecting Psychological Symptoms of Brain-Injury." *Exceptional Children,* 28: 57–62 (September, 1961).

Black, Millard H., "Characteristics of the Culturally Disadvantaged Child," in Joe L. Frost and Glenn R. Hawkes, eds., *The Disadvantaged Child.* Boston, Houghton Mifflin, 1966, pp. 45–50.

Blackham, Garth J., *The Deviant Child in the Classroom.* Belmont, Calif., Wadsworth, 1967.

Bower, Eli M., and Lambert, Nadine M., "In-School Screening of Children with Emotional Handicaps," in Nicholas J. Long, William C. Morse, and Ruth G. Newman, eds., *Conflict in the Classroom.* Belmont, Calif., Wadsworth, 1966, pp. 128–34.

Bower, Eli M., "Comparison of the Characteristics of Identified Emotionally Disturbed Children with Other Children in Classes," in E. Philip Trapp and Philip Himelstein, eds., *Readings on the Exceptional Child.* New York, Appleton-Century-Crofts, 1962, pp. 610–28.

Bradley, Charles, "Organic Factors in the Psychopathology of Childhood," in Paul H. Hoch and Joseph Zubin, eds., *Psychopathology of Childhood.* New York, Grune & Stratton, 1955, pp. 82–104.

Clark, Kenneth, "Rejected Minority Group Children," in James F. Magary and John R. Eichorn, eds., *The Exceptional Child: A Book of Readings.* New York, Holt, Rinehart & Winston, 1962, pp. 46–65.

Clements, Sam D., *Minimal Brain Dysfunction in Children: Terminology and Identification.* (Phase one of a three-phase project), National Institute of Neurological Diseases and Blindness, Monograph No. 3. Washington, D.C., U.S. Department of Health, Education and Welfare, 1966.

Cohn, Robert, and Nardini, John E., "The Correlation of Bilateral Occipital Slow Activity in the Human E.E.G. with Certain Disorders of Behavior," *American Journal of Psychiatry,* 115: 44–54 (July, 1958).

Cruickshank, William M., Bentzen, Florence A., Ratzeburg, Frederick H., and Tannhauser, Mirian F., *A Teaching Method for Brain-Injured and Hyperactive Children.* Syracuse, N.Y., Syracuse University Press, 1961.

Dunn, Lloyd M., *Exceptional Children in the School.* New York, Holt, Rinehart & Winston, 1963.

Dunsing, Jack D., and Kephart, Newell C., "Motor Generalizations in Space and Time," in Jerome Hellmuth, ed., *Learning Disorders,* Vol. I. Seattle, Wash., Seattle Sequin School, Special Child Publications, 1965.

Enstrom, E. A., "Handwriting for the Retarded: Out of the Classroom." *Exceptional Children,* 32: 385–88 (February, 1966).

Epps, Helen O., McCammon, Gertrude B., and Simmons, Queen O., *Teaching Devices for Children with Impaired Learning.* Columbus, Ohio, The Parents' Volunteer Association-Columbus State School, 1958.

Freedman, Sanford J., Grunebaum, Henry U., and Greenblatt, Milton, "Perceptive and Cognitive Changes in Sensory Deprivation," in Philip Solomon, et al., eds., *Sensory Deprivation: A Symposium Held at Harvard Medical School.* Cambridge, Mass., Harvard University Press, 1961.

Freidus, Elizabeth, "New Approaches in Special Education of the Brain-Injured Child," in *The "Brain-Injured" Child.* New York, New York Association for Brain Injured Children, n.d., pp. 14–18.

Fremont, Herbert, "Some Thoughts on Teaching Mathematics to Disadvantaged Groups," in Joe L. Frost and Glenn R. Hawkes, eds., *The Disadvantaged Child.* Boston, Houghton Mifflin, 1966, pp. 316–23.

Frost, Joe L., and Hawkes, Glenn R., "The Disadvantaged Child: Overview and Recommendations," in *The Disadvantaged Child.* Boston, Houghton Mifflin, 1966.

Frostig, Marianne, and Horne, David, "Assessment of Visual Perception and Its Importance in Education." *The A.A.M.D. Education Reporter,* 2: 11–12 (April, 1962).

Frostig, Marianne, and Horne, David, *The Frostig Program for the Development of Visual Perception: Teacher's Guide.* Chicago, Follett, 1964.

Gardner, Richard, "Psychogenic Problems of Brain-Injured Children and Their Parents." *Journal of American Academy of Child Psychiatry,* Vol. 7, No. 3 (July, 1968), pp. 471–91.

Getman, G. N., *How to Develop Your Child's Intelligence.* Luverne, Minn., the author, 1962.

Goldstein, Kurt, and Sheerer, Martin, *Abstract and Concrete Behavior: An Experimental Study with Special Tests.* Psychological Monographs of American Psychological Associations, Vol. 53, No. 2, Washington, D.C., 1941.

Gotkin, Lassar G., "A Calendar Curriculum for Disadvantaged Kinder-

garten Children." *Teachers' College Record,* Vol. LXVII, No. 5 (February, 1967), pp. 406–417.
Graver, Palmer A., "Facilitating the Results of Therapy," in James F. Magary and John R. Eichorn, eds., *The Exceptional Child: A Book of Readings.* New York, Holt, Rinehart & Winston, 1962, pp. 374–80.
Gray, Doris, "The Blind Child in the Regular Classroom," in James F. Magary and John R. Eichorn, eds., *The Exceptional Child: A Book of Readings.* New York, Holt, Rinehart & Winston, 1962, pp. 258–66.
Haring, Norris G., and Whelan, Richard J., "Experimental Methods in Education and Management," in Nicholas J. Long, William C. Morse, and Ruth G. Newman, eds., *Conflict in the Classroom.* Belmont, Calif., Wadsworth, 1966, pp. 389–404.
Harper, Louis E., and Wright, Benjamin, "Dealing with Emotional Problems in the Classroom," in James F. Magary and John R. Eichorn, eds., *The Exceptional Child: A Book of Readings.* New York, Holt, Rinehart & Winston, 1962, pp. 354–67.
Haubrich, Vernon F., "The Culturally Disadvantaged and Teacher Education," in Joe L. Frost and Glenn R. Hawkes, eds., *The Disadvantaged Child.* Boston, Houghton Mifflin, 1966, pp. 362–68.
Havighurst, Robert J., "Who Are the Socially Disadvantaged?" in Joe L. Frost and Glenn R. Hawkes, eds., *The Disadvantaged Child.* Boston, Houghton Mifflin, 1966, pp. 15–23.
Humphrey, George, "The Problem of Generalization." *Bulletin of Canadian Psychological Association,* Vol. 4, No. 3 (October, 1944), pp. 37–51.
Jacobson, Stanley, and Faegre, Christopher, "Neutralization: A Tool for the Teacher of Disturbed Children." *Exceptional Children,* 25: 243–46 (February, 1959).
Johnson, Doris J., and Myklebust, Helmer R., *Learning Disabilities: Educational Principles and Practices.* New York, Grune & Stratton, 1967.
Johnson, Orville G., *Education for the Slow Learner.* Englewood Cliffs, N.J., Prentice-Hall, 1963.
Jordan, Thomas E., *The Exceptional Child.* Columbus, Ohio, Charles E. Merrill, 1962.
Kirk, Samuel A., *Educating Exceptional Children.* Boston, Houghton Mifflin, 1962.
Knickerbocker, Major Barbara M., "The Significance of Body Schema and Body Image in Perceptual Motor Dysfunction," in *Proceedings: Ohio Occupational Therapy Association 1966 Conference: Body Image.* Cleveland, Ohio, 1966.
Kough, Jack, and De Haan, Robert F., *Identifying Children with Special Needs,* Vol. I. Chicago, Science Research Associates, 1955.
Kreuter, Mortimer, "A Public School in a Correctional Institution." *Federal Probation,* September, 1965, pp. 50–57.

Krippner, Stanley, "Sociopathic Tendencies and Reading Retardation in Children." *Exceptional Children*, 29: 258–66 (February, 1963).

Krupp, George R., and Schwartzberg, Bernard, "The Brain-Injured Child: A Challenge to Social Workers." *Social Casework*, 41: 63–69 (February, 1960).

Landis, Carney, and Bolles, M. Marjorie, *Textbook of Abnormal Psychology*. New York, Macmillan, 1947.

Lent, John E., "Helping Stutterers in the Classroom," in James F. Magary and John R. Eichorn, eds., *The Exceptional Child: A Book of Readings*. New York, Holt, Rinehart & Winston, 1962, pp. 327–29.

Long, Nicholas J., Morse, William C., and Newman, Ruth G., *Conflict in the Classroom*. Belmont, Calif., Wadsworth, 1966.

Pate, John E., "Emotionally Disturbed and Socially Maladjusted Children," in Lloyd M. Dunn, ed., *Exceptional Children in the Schools*. New York, Holt, Rinehart & Winston, 1963, pp. 239–84.

Pelone, Anthony J., "The Adjustment of the Partially Seeing Child in the Regular Classroom," in James F. Magary and John R. Eichorn, eds., *The Exceptional Child: A Book of Readings*. New York, Holt, Rinehart & Winston, 1962, pp. 270–79.

Peter, Laurence J., *Prescriptive Teaching*. New York, McGraw-Hill, 1965.

Redl, Fritz, and Wineman, David, *The Aggressive Child*. New York, The Free Press, 1957.

Rhodes, William C., "Curriculum and Disordered Behavior," in Nicholas J. Long, William C. Morse, and Ruth G. Newman, eds., *Conflict in the Classroom*. Belmont, Calif., Wadsworth, 1966, pp. 405–10.

Riessman, Frank, *The Culturally Deprived Child*. New York, Harper & Row, 1962.

Rosen, Irving M., "Development of Body Image," in *Proceedings: Ohio Occupational Therapy Association 1966 Conference: Body Image*. Cleveland, Ohio, 1966.

Rosenberg, Sheldon, "Problem Solving and Conceptual Behavior," in Norman R. Ellis, ed., *Handbook of Mental Deficiency: Psychological Theory and Research*. New York, McGraw-Hill, 1963, pp. 439–59.

Sarason, Seymour B., *Psychological Problems in Mental Deficiency*. New York, Harper & Brothers, 1959.

Siegel, Ernest, *Helping the Brain Injured Child*. New York, New York Association for Brain Injured Children, 1961.

Siegel, Ernest, Gisonti, Frank, and Posnack, Gerald, *Who Said It?: A Teaching Aid in Communication*. Freeport, N.Y., Educational Activities, 1965.

Siegel, Ernest, "Integrating Handicapped Children and Youth into Regular Religious Educational Programs." *Religious Education*, Vol. LXII, No. 4 (July–August, 1967), pp. 355–57.

Strauss, Alfred, and Lehtinen, Laura, *Psychopathology and Education of the Brain-Injured Child*, Vol. I. New York, Grune & Stratton, 1947.

Strauss, Alfred A., and Kephart, Newell C., *Psychopathology and Education of the Brain-Injured Child,* Vol. II. New York, Grune & Stratton, 1955.
Streng, Alice, "The Child Who Is Hard of Hearing," in James F. Magary and John R. Eichorn, eds., *The Exceptional Child: A Book of Readings.* New York, Holt, Rinehart & Winston, 1962.
Ullmann, Leonard B., and Krasner, Leonard, *Case Studies in Behavior Modifications.* New York, Holt, Rinehart & Winston, 1965.
Webster's New Twentieth Century Dictionary of the English Language— Unabridged. New York, Standard Reference Works Publishing Co., 1956.
Woltman, Adolph G., "The Use of Puppetry in Therapy," in Nicholas J. Long, William C. Morse, and Ruth G. Newman, eds., *Conflict in the Classroom.* Belmont, Calif., Wadsworth, 1966, pp. 202–208.
Zeaman, David, and House, Betty J., "The Role of Attention in Retardate Discrimination Learning," in Norman J. Ellis, ed., *Handbook of Mental Deficiency: Psychological Theory and Research.* New York, McGraw-Hill, 1963.

CHAPTER

4

Additional Aspects of the Teacher's Role

Assisting in Identification

It is generally agreed that early identification of the handicapped is essential if they are to attain optimal adjustment. Often a learning and/or a behavior problem (as well as some purely physical problems) can be treated in the early stages with a much greater degree of effectiveness and with far less specialized help (Mase 1962: 341). Also, detection—and diagnosis—may suggest specific modifications of classroom methodology, special techniques and approaches and, even more important, may be instrumental in fostering a change of teacher attitude to one more in consonance with the child's educational and emotional needs. A slow learner is less likely to be judged by the teacher as "lazy," "ornery," "willful" or "negatively motivated" if, through diagnosis, the factor of mental retardation becomes evident. If detected, the child can be referred to various services (*e.g.,* a mildly retarded child might be referred to a special social/recreational after-school group; an emotionally disturbed child may be referred for counseling; a minimally brain-injured child may be referred to an optometrist for visual training). Knowing the child's true handicap, the teacher might be helpful in effecting a different class placement—per-

Additional Aspects of the Teacher's Role

haps in a "slower" regular class, a smaller class or even a special class.

The teacher's role in the identification process is one of referral rather than of labeling. A teacher would not tell a child that he has measles; he would notice the symptoms and refer the child to the school nurse. Similarly, a teacher would not tell a child's parent that he suspects that the youngster has a neurological impairment; he would observe the possible manifestations of this condition (distractibility, perseveration, lack of coordination, disorganization, etc.) and would refer the child to the proper source—school principal, school nurse or doctor, guidance counselor or school psychologist. Despite this "chain of command" recommendation, it should be pointed out that experienced classroom teachers do become reasonably proficient in recognizing specific areas of exceptionality. Bower (1957) found that the classroom teachers' judgments—that is, recognition—of emotional disturbances are remarkably similar to the level of reliability of clinicians.

The teacher's skill in recognizing the pupil who is in need of referral is a function of his experience and training. Through teacher-training programs prior to teaching appointment, in-service training, reading, workshops and conferences, etc., the conscientious teacher can become acquainted with the identifying characteristics of exceptional children.

At times, certain disadvantages may obtain as a result of diagnosing. For example, one hears the cry "Don't label the child mentally retarded; there is a stigma attached to that term." Isn't it likely, though, that the stigma attaches itself to the *child* rather than to the *term?* After all, he behaves differently, is perceived as different by society. Instead of engendering warmth, sympathy and compassion, these differences all too often evoke rejection, intolerance, even cruelty.

There are other possible negative concomitants in the diagnostic process. Among those mentioned by Wolfensberger (1965) are:

1. Diagnosis is often a dead end for the family in that instead of leading to a trafficking toward meaningful services, it may result in only a "frustrating series of fruitless cross-referrals." Moreover, not only does diagnostic evaluation sometimes fail to lead to a service; it may actually result in the exclusion of the child from programs in which he was formerly enrolled.

2. Diagnostic centers often fail to provide adequate feedback counseling to the parent, despite the fact that parents are often expected to accept the final decision of the diagnostic team.

3. There is frequently an abundance of diagnostic facilities in comparison with other available resources. The existence of these centers masks the need for additional services since they themselves are regarded as "services." This is analogous to a patient who, having had his temperature taken, does not seek therapy, in the mistaken belief that taking one's temperature constitutes a "medicine."

4. Early diagnosis can be a disaster in that it may precipitate a premature, incorrect decision on the part of the child's family (*e.g.*, institutionalization), whereas if the diagnosing, *i.e.*, labeling, had not occurred, the child might have experienced greater parental acceptance.

Added to this would be the rare cases of misuse and actual abuse of information—the teacher who calls a child "crazy" upon learning that he is undergoing psychotherapy; the teacher who, upon learning that a child is mentally retarded, refers to him as a "dummy" and refrains from trying to teach him any meaningful academic subject matter, etc.

The foregoing examples of possible negative consequences of diagnosis, flying as they do in the face of the general consensus of authorities who plead for early diagnosis, warrant a somber pause. The question of whether or not it is better to diagnose is essentially an empty query. It would be more thoughtful for the classroom teacher to address himself to such questions as:

"When and why shall I initiate a diagnosis?" (*i.e.*, "Are his symptoms significant?")

Additional Aspects of the Teacher's Role

"How can I best use the diagnostic information?" (*i.e.,* "Can I translate it into specific classroom techniques?")

"Are further referrals in order?" (*i.e.,* "On the basis of my classroom observation plus the diagnostic nomenclature, are further *services*—not additional diagnoses—needed?")

Regarding the possibility that a teacher might abuse diagnostic information, one must immediately ask how effective this teacher was *prior* to becoming acquainted with the pupil's diagnosis. It seems a safe assumption that such maladjusted teachers (certainly rare) would be ineffective and harmful to children generally, regardless of the case history information they may possess.

> There are isolated cases of malpractice in medicine, of psychologists who administer and interpret tests incorrectly, of counselors who offer unsound advice, of teachers who mistreat a child despite learning—or perhaps because of learning—that the child has a handicap. To condemn *all* professionals because of this incompetent minority is illogical and unscientific, a completely negative and unworkable approach.
>
> If any of the manifestations of the child's handicap are at all significant (although, perhaps, not obvious), then it would seem that the professional who works with this child should know of the condition. He will then be able to relate to the child more effectively, understand him more fully and help him meet more of his needs. He will be in a better position to guide the group in accepting and helping this child. There are, of course, exceptions to every rule, but, by and large, one must assume competency on the part of professionals [Siegel 1961: 82].*

In a broad sense, the mildly handicapped child in a regular classroom who demonstrates significant (albeit mild) learning and/or behavior impairment has already been diagnosed—that is, *he is different; he has problems; he performs less adequately than his peers.* The specific diagnosis merely explains *why*.

* Reprinted with permission from *Helping the Brain Injured Child,* New York Association for Brain Injured Children, 1961.

Gathering and Sharing Information

The regular classroom teacher can help the mildly handicapped child more fully and systematically if he adheres to sound record-keeping procedures. The two chief purposes for information gathering seem to be the following:

A. Committing oneself to the policy of effective information-gathering procedures, in a sense, commits the teacher more fully to the child—that is, he virtually is compelled to become more aware of him, his strengths and weaknesses, his needs and limitations, his life style and coping mechanisms, etc., as he gathers pertinent data (written notes as well as mental notes and impressions) about the child.

B. Since the process of information gathering is an ongoing and dynamic one, rather than simply a single action, it can help the teacher to evaluate pupil progress. Seen in this light, record keeping is the "research" instrument whereby the teacher can test various hypotheses dealing with materials, methods and approaches.

Some specific techniques and instruments for information gathering have been suggested by the New York City Board of Education (1955: 157–267). They include observation and recording, interviews with child as well as with parent, tests and measurements, the sociogram and other projective techniques such as dramatics, play, puppetry and art.

It is important that information about the child be shared by the various professional school personnel who come in contact with him. One example of this would be the child's current teacher getting information from his former teacher. Another illustration might be the case of a junior high school home room teacher seeking out a subject teacher (*e.g.*, the gym teacher) to discuss ways in which he might help alleviate a minimally brain-injured child's coordination problem; pointing out to the music teacher that an emotionally disturbed child who happens to excel in music should receive excessive praise in an effort to strengthen his self-concept; alerting the woodwork shop teacher to a mildly mentally retarded child who is talented in shop but is sensitive about not being able to read with ease the shop safety signs, charts and various printed instructions.

In addition to fellow teachers, the teacher should become involved with other school personnel—principal, assistant principal, school doctor, nurse, guidance counselor, school psychologist—regarding the gathering and sharing of information.

Utilizing Supportive Services

A mildly handicapped child in a regular classroom may have specific problems that require the services of a specialist outside the classroom, sometimes even outside the school. These supportive services include:

SPEECH TEACHERS. Some mildly handicapped children may require the services of a speech teacher. A brain-injured child may have organic articulatory problems or auditory perceptual difficulties which require special speech and hearing training. All three categories—emotionally disturbed, mentally retarded and brain-injured—may present problems in communication (not addressing oneself to the point, speaking too rapidly, interrupting, difficulty in listening, rambling, etc.).

PSYCHOTHERAPIST (OR COUNSELOR). The basic needs of the emotionally disturbed are a greater acceptance of reality, development of insight and strengthening of ego functions (Johnson and Myklebust 1967: 55). By definition, then, this group of exceptional children can benefit from the intervention of some kind of psychotherapeutic agent. Similarly, the anxiety and low self-esteem of the brain-injured and the mentally retarded can be viewed as emotional maladjustment—the so-called "overlays" of emotional disturbance. Whether we are talking about classical Freudian analysis, group therapy, play therapy, counseling, etc., it seems reasonable to assume that some form of supportive counseling is required by many of the learning and/or behaviorally impaired.

VISUAL TRAINING SPECIALIST. The brain-injured usually suffer from visual perceptual impairment; the emotionally disturbed may also evidence visual perceptual disturbances, albeit psychogenically based; mental retardation, too, is at times coupled with some sensory-perceptual deficits. Children from all three categories can, at times, benefit from special visual perceptual training (Getman 1962; Frostig and Horne 1965).

PRIVATE TUTORING. Many children who manifest learning problems are often helped by private tutoring that augments the group learning program (Gallagher 1960; Bender 1953; Bower 1960: 236). It is logical to view this in purely educational terms—that is, children who have some difficulty in the learning process may need the repetition, the rephrasing, the additional experience, the "tailor-made" systematic approach of the private tutor (remedial reading specialist, educational therapist or others). Besides the educational compensation of a tutoring program, therapeutic benefits have also been listed (Goldberg 1952).

OTHER SUPPORTIVE SERVICES. Other examples of supportive services are music therapy, art therapy and occupational therapy, which have psychotherapeutic effects as well as pure "subject matter" gains in music, art and the use of the hands; physiotherapy for some children who present neurological disorders; vocational guidance and social adjustment groups for some of the older learning and/or behaviorally impaired children.

The classroom teacher is not always the logical person to make the direct referral. In many cases, he may suspect that a particular service is warranted, but he would be more judicious in referring indirectly (*e.g.,* the teacher may wish to refer the child to the school psychologist who, in turn, may make the referral for ongoing therapy; he may wish to refer the child to

the school doctor before recommending visual training, etc.).
In fact, there is a relationship between a teacher referral and
the existence of a diagnosis, case history, confidential folder, etc.
Usually, early detection and initiation of *diagnosis* precedes a
referral to a specialized service. In short, it is best to know what
the problem is before prescribing for its amelioration.

The fact that these specialized services exist does not prevent
the teacher from offering *some* of the supportive service in the
classroom. Teachers can—and do—offer some speech correction,
visual training and occupational therapy (often by means of
arts and crafts) in the classroom. Also, despite the difference in
opinion over whether the teacher's role should be that of
teacher or of therapist, it is generally agreed—and, indeed,
fervently hoped—that the teacher and the classroom experiences
have a therapeutic effect on the child.

Teachers (and administrators) who are secure will not view
the referral of a child for supportive services as an indictment
against themselves for not doing their jobs adequately. This
does happen at times, particularly with regard to the service of
private tutoring—"After all, if the school is doing its job, why
should the child require additional teaching?" The secure
teacher recognizes the fact that some children with learning
blocks, perceptual disturbances, difficulty in abstract thinking,
deficiencies in transfer of learning and relatively meager incidental learning prowess can benefit from one-to-one instruction.
The need of these children for additional specialized teaching is
in no way a reflection upon the classroom teacher's capabilities.

As with all good things, one must avoid surfeiting. It is
possible for overanxious parents, in their zeal to make their
child as "normal" as possible as quickly as possible, to overservice the child. In these cases, the classroom teacher—perhaps
in conjunction with other professionals—assists the parents in
deciding which of the proliferation of services are needed at
that given moment, and which should be held in abeyance.

Participation in In-Service Training

The regular classroom teacher, having majored in elementary education or in a subject area and secondary education, is in a real sense not prepared to teach the exceptional child. Yet regular classes usually have one or more children who are mildly, yet significantly, handicapped, thereby requiring a "special education" approach (*i.e.*, understanding of the nature and needs of children falling in a specific category of exceptionality, an ability to translate this knowledge into appropriate methodology, individualization, etc.). Many special education courses are offered at local teacher-training institutions; in addition, boards of education often establish and conduct in-service courses geared specifically to the needs of their teachers. Also available are workshops, demonstration courses and professional libraries. With increasing frequency, conferences and conventions are being sponsored by professional organizations (Council for Exceptional Children, American Association on Mental Deficiency, The Orton Society, American Association for Orthopsychiatry, etc.), state departments of education, universities and medical colleges, private schools and parent groups (New York Association for Brain Injured Children, Association for Children with Learning Disabilities, United Cerebral Palsy, National Organization for Mentally Ill Children, Association for the Help of Retarded Children, and others). These conferences serve several purposes: (1) They bring current research and innovations (local, national and even international) to the attention of the teacher. (2) They serve the "psychological" function of enabling the teacher to identify with the field of special education. (3) They dramatize to the teacher the importance of his role. (4) They are, per se, an example of interdisciplinary functioning, thereby making the teacher aware of the roles of other professionals and emphasizing the concept of "the whole child." (5) They serve as a platform

Additional Aspects of the Teacher's Role 117

whereby the teacher, acting as a participant, can share his views and experiences with others. (6) Finally, the change of pace and of scenery, the aura of "glamour," the opportunity to mingle with renowned authorities (professional celebrities of a sort) can bring to the teacher renewed stamina, enthusiasm and dedication.

An important function of teacher-training programs is that they often serve to shape teachers' attitudes toward the handicapped. The attitude of the classroom teacher toward children suffering from learning and/or behavior problems is paramount. Even in cases of severe mental illness, the attitude of those coming in contact with the patient is an essential treatment ingredient, and in fact, a particular kind of attitude is sometimes stipulated. Lamm and Folsom (1965) prescribe five attitudes: (1) *kind firmness* for the depressed, (2) *active friendliness* for the withdrawn, apathetic schizophrenic, (3) *passive friendliness* for the paranoid patient who fears closeness, (4) *matter-of-factness* for the manipulator (*i.e.*, certain character disorders), and (5) *no demand* for the patient in uncontrollable, global rage.

Certainly, it would be impossible to prescribe a particular teacher attitude to match a particular etiology. However, it is safe to say that mildly handicapped children in the regular classroom—particularly those with learning and/or behavior impairments—all need a supportive and accepting teacher attitude. Kough and De Haan (1957: 168) believe that if the teacher's "attitude toward the youngsters is positive, if [teachers] accept the handicap as a limitation that can be overcome, [they] will communicate . . . [their] feelings to the youngsters and help generate a spirit of confidence. . . ."

Research shows that special class teachers of retarded children place greater emphasis on personal and social adjustment and make relatively fewer academic demands than do regular teachers (Fine 1967). What accounts for this difference in attitude between regular and special class teachers? Perhaps one explanation is lack of preparation, which results in lack of knowhow in terms of understanding and teaching exceptional children. It may very well be that philosophical tenets generally encountered in regular teacher-training courses—"Each child is an individual," "Don't teach arithmetic—teach the child," "Children are not only intellectual, but they are physical, social and emotional as well" (the concept of the "whole child")—while helpful in providing the regular classroom teacher with insights into *normal* children, are inadequate—even platitudinous—when applied to *handicapped* children. More specifics are needed. Can it be that the regular classroom teacher, "plagued" with a few exceptional children, not understanding them and feeling ineffective in teaching them or in bringing about behavioral modifications, begins to feel frustrated, insecure and threatened? Further, is it possible that these feelings give way to fear of and hostility toward these handicapped children? Anthropologists (Kluckhohn 1944: 231, 237) tell us that a certain amount of security for oneself is necessary before one develops respect for others, and that those who are themselves insecure manifest hostility toward others. Is it not possible, then, that the regular teacher, having developed a feeling of insecurity arising out of his inability to deal effectively with the problem child in his classroom, lashes out—often unconsciously—at the source of his frustration and feelings of inadequacy—*i.e.*, the handicapped child?

In-service training (often including demonstrations and workshops—*i.e.*, the opportunity to work with handicapped children) can provide the teacher with insight into the problems of the handicapped child and can suggest techniques that might be instrumental in helping him in the classroom. This armamentarium of knowledge can go a long way in effecting a teacher attitude that is conducive to the education and to the emotional well-being of the child. Ratchik and Koenig (1963: 18, 19) state that negative teacher attitudes can often be changed by means of "an understanding of the nature of the child's handicap and the manner in which it might affect daily behavior."

Finally, the very timing of in-service training is a tremendously important factor. All too often, undergraduates complain that education courses are taught "in a vacuum," because they are taught vicariously *about* children but are not given sufficient firsthand experience with children. Some attempt is made to remedy the situation by providing films and other audiovisual aids depicting children, guided visits and observations, workshops and, finally, student-teaching experiences. However, there is a world of difference between any of these (even student teaching) and actual teaching. The classroom teacher has sole responsibility for his pupils—he is "in the trenches," so to speak. The problems that he brings to in-service courses are real, vital and urgent—an example of intrinsic motivation at its highest. Viewed in the light of "on-the-job training," special education in-service courses can be beneficial to all teachers, even the special education majors.

Lesson Planning

The construction of daily lesson plans can, in itself, be an important factor in the growth of the handicapped child in the regular classroom. In a sense, planning commits the teacher to consider the handicapped child, to anticipate the effect the lesson will have upon him, to devise modifications which are feasible for regular classroom use and beneficial to the individual child.

There are many variations of acceptable lesson plan forms. All, however, contain certain common elements: *e.g.,* aim, motivation, activities, development, materials, content, evaluation. These are important for all children, but seem to have special significance for the handicapped child in the regular classroom. Normal children are able to learn a great deal incidentally. Therefore, even if the aim of the lesson isn't quite clear, perhaps these children can distinguish the trivial from the essential by noting the teacher's facial expressions or tone of voice. But mentally retarded children have difficulty in incidental learning, and brain-injured children are often lacking in "social perception," unable to siphon meaning and significance out of the facial expression and behavior of others (Johnson and Myklebust 1967: 34, 46); therefore, the clarity of the aim is essential to them. Normal children, generally encountering pleasurable experiences at school, are often intrinsically motivated to learn, whereas learning and/or behaviorally impaired children, having experienced defeat both in and out of school, may require meaningful, planned and additional motivation. Similarly, the development of the lesson, important for the entire class, is of even greater significance for the exceptional child in the regular class; this becomes clear when we consider such factors in lesson development as sequence, tempo, variety of activities, dosages, etc.

Treatman (1957: 157) suggests to supervisors that a lesson's aim should be developed cooperatively and that it should be appropriate, worthwhile, challenging, clear, understood, definite, significant and (hopefully) realized; the motivation of the lesson should be sustained, personalized (even emotionalized), intrinsic, rooted in experience and suitable to the age and maturity of the group. Each of these stipulations, while written in terms of all children, have obvious and direct relevance to the education of the mildly handicapped child in the regular classroom.

Siegel (1967) has enumerated some suggestions for developing effective lessons. This list* was compiled specifically for teachers of minimally brain-injured and emotionally disturbed children enrolled in a private school (The Adams School, New York City), but it can be of equal importance to the teacher of the mildly handicapped child in the regular classroom:

* Reprinted with permission of The Adams School, New York, N.Y.

1. Plan fully (written plans): materials, activities, lesson development (*i.e.*, sequence of activities). Daily plan of lesson should dovetail with long-range plans (syllabus, scope).
2. Plan for a variety of meaningful activities. Each lesson should include some independent work. (Upper classes, especially, should include more written work.) Doses should be small and the parts unified.
3. Continuity is important. Refer to past lessons, future plans, homework.
4. Motivation is important. Where possible, children should see need for the lesson—this enhances interest and cooperation. Often audiovisual aids help. Hint: Motivation should "shake up" the children.
5. Be fully aware of the time. Lessons should not end merely because the bell rings. *Planned* endings are important (summary, review, evaluation). Plan fully and have certain brief, optional activities on hand.
6. Each lesson should end on a cohesive, definitive, high-interest note. (If individual or group work is done, *all* children should be brought back to a common theme.) Try to develop in each child a sense of belonging to the class.
7. The aim of the lesson should be *appropriate* (to the age and ability of each student); *clear* (to teacher, pupils and observers); and *suitable*. Be aware of auxiliary aims as well (*e.g.*, perceptual training, visual-motor activities, conceptualization tasks, etc.).
8. Keep a record of progress (a corollary of plans) that is both brief and individualized.
9. Allow children at times to share in the planning—to be aware of the lesson's aim. Do not let things "just happen" to the child.

Relationships with Parents

At times, teachers of learning and/or behaviorally impaired children rate their parents on the basis of how "good" they are in staying away from—and therefore not "bothering"—the school. On the other hand, parents of these children may have negative mental sets which either keep them away from school or, if they do visit the school, render them ineffective in establishing fruitful parent-teacher relations.

Wright (1960: 288–96) considered negative attitudes, which might exist on the part of both the teacher and the parents of handicapped children, which would militate against harmonious, constructive team effort. The interfering parental attitudes listed were: fear or awe of the teacher as the authority figure; fear of being blamed for the child's difficulties; suspicion that the situation might require an excessive amount of time, energy and money; fear of impatience on the part of the teacher in not being able to understand the parent's concern with making the child "normal"; fear that the teacher will shatter the last slim hope that the parent holds out for the child's improvement or, conversely, a fear that the teacher will not "level" with the parent in that the worst aspects of the child's shortcomings won't be discussed; fear that the child may become "too attached"—too emotionally dependent upon the teacher. The interfering teacher attitudes mentioned were: the automatic assignment of blame for the child's condition to the parent; the refusal to share decision-making responsibilities with the parent; and a feeling of discomfort or even revulsion when placed in the presence of handicapped children. To these might be added the fear that the parent may be too critical of the teacher's efforts, blaming him for not being able to bring the child up to the parent's expectations of "normalcy," and resentment of the parent's unrealistic attitude.

What is needed is mutual confidence, respect and empathy. In the majority of cases, both teachers and parents are working toward the same goal—the development and adjustment of the child. However, their efforts are hampered because of inability to communicate and subsequent defensive thinking. Timing is an important ingredient in communication. All too often, the parent visits the school after six or seven months have elapsed only to learn for the first time that his child "is the worst I've

Additional Aspects of the Teacher's Role

ever seen" or "he will never make it next year and will have to be retained." Clearly, it would have been more logical to consult with the parent during the early part of the term, when cooperative efforts could perhaps have effected some improvement. Similarly, it sometimes happens that a parent visits a school to question or even complain of some practice or policy which he believes affects his child's well-being. At this time, he may be asked, "Would you consider a special class for your child?" The parent may then feel that if the teacher or principal really believed that a special class would be the optimal placement, this opinion should have been conveyed earlier, and independently—not as a countermove to a parent complaint. The poor timing, then, may be the sole factor which leads the parent to mistrust the teacher and to suspect his motivation. Thus, a fear of "punitive placement" may develop, whereby parents suspect teachers, administrators and school systems generally and fear a retaliatory policy: "If you keep bothering us, we can put your child in a class for mentally retarded." A tendency may thus develop on the part of the parents to "let well enough alone," lest their suggestions and questions be regarded as complaints.

Needless to say, these fears are usually ungrounded, but it will require direct effort on the part of the school personnel—particularly the teacher—to convince the parents that they, their views, their knowledge of their children are indeed welcome. Even in cases (as with some emotionally disturbed children) where it is obvious that the parents are the source of the difficulty, the teacher should still include the parents in joint efforts directed toward the well-being of the child (Morse 1958: 594–95). In other words, granted that the classroom teacher is dedicated to helping the handicapped child, the factor of an ineffective, even harmful parent is not a signal to the teacher to abandon his endeavors—it merely renders his job more difficult.

The teacher must learn to cope with the overanxious parents, the ones who find problems where, in fact, none exist and who interject their own anxieties into otherwise normal classroom situations. These parents may be helped through general educational programs for parents (PTA, etc.), school specialists available for consultation or ongoing counseling and therapy sessions (Morse 1958: 595).

Wright (1960: 289) has proposed some guideposts in establishing positive parent-school relationships (these can serve as yardsticks, enabling the school to evaluate its effectiveness in communicating to the parent its positive motivations):

- The parent must feel that the teacher is not working against him, and that, jointly, they are endeavoring to find answers to the common problem.
- The teacher must be able to convey to the parent that he likes the child, respects him as an individual and understands—even enjoys—his personality.
- The teacher must be able to communicate to the parent that he recognizes his strengths and the fact that he is "doing all he can" to help his child; shortcomings of the parents may be noted by the teacher, but the parent must be made to feel that these shortcomings are not magnified by the teacher and do not result in rejection.

There are many specific areas that are best served by teacher-parent cooperation: If the child is on medication, the teacher should be informed of this by the parent so that he might know what to expect (drowsiness, for example); moreover, the teacher might be able to help evaluate the drug's effectiveness. The parent can inform the teacher of the child's interests and hobbies, fears, particular areas of emotional sensitivity, etc. The teacher, in turn, can elicit the parents' cooperation in such areas as speech exercises and visual training.

In addition, the parent can be helpful in supervision of homework assignments, in preparing the child for school in terms of appropriate clothing, organization of books and school supplies, and punctuality. These areas are particularly relevant to the learning and/or behaviorally impaired. Brain-injured

Additional Aspects of the Teacher's Role

children are generally disorganized and need a superimposed structure. Mentally retarded children—often experiencing difficulty with incidental learning and with transfer of learning—may require the specific instruction and guidance by the parent. Emotionally disturbed children may also benefit from this additional parental attention and support. Nonhandicapped children frequently can fend for themselves in these areas, but handicapped children, by virtue of their physical and/or emotional limitations, are more likely to require parents' supervision.

(Note: This is not to say that all parents are equipped to work with their children. Some, being too emotionally involved, become nervous, tense and hostile when supervising and correcting their child; the child, in turn, becomes more anxious and fearful. Through counseling, such parents can gain insight into their own feelings and learn to accept their child's limitations. The skillful teacher may be able to select a minimum of responsibilities for these parents—responsibilities that are sufficient to make them feel positively involved with their children, yet are neutral, nominal and psychologically safe. Many parents, however, are well-adjusted, able and willing to work with their child. The classroom teacher should utilize these parents' cooperation, energies and attitudes.)

In addition to working cooperatively with an individual parent, the classroom teacher may become active in parent organizations. In so doing, parents and teacher have an opportunity to learn each other's views and to work together for the handicapped children involved. The teacher's becoming a member of the parent organization can thus be viewed as both a cause and effect of positive parent-teacher relations. Often, the regular classroom teacher can help the mildly handicapped child in his class by becoming active in the school's Parent-Teacher Association. Here, the parents of the normal children can become acquainted with the problems of the exceptional child. The teacher, by suggesting that some of the PTA programs be devoted to the topic of exceptional children, may be instrumental in effecting a more positive attitude toward the handicapped. After all, attending these meetings are the neighbors of the learning and/or behaviorally impaired child. Perhaps, a greater awareness of the handicapped child, his strengths and weaknesses, and a focusing upon the role of the public in effecting optimal adjustment, can truly create a more enlightened public—enlightened in action as well as in knowledge.

REFERENCES

Bender, Lauretta, "Childhood Schizophrenia." *Psychiatric Quarterly,* Vol. 27, No. 4 (October, 1953), pp. 663–81.

Bower, Eli M., "A Process for Identifying Disturbed Children." *Children,* 4: 143–47 (July, 1957).

Bower, Eli M., "Emotionally Handicapped Child and the School." *Exceptional Children,* 26: 233–42 (January, 1960).

Fine, Marvin J., "Attitudes of Regular and Special Teachers Toward the Educable Mentally Retarded Child." *Exceptional Children,* Vol. 33, No. 6 (February, 1967), pp. 429–30.

Frostig, Marianne, and Horne, David, "An Approach to the Treatment of Children with Learning Disorders," in Jerome Hellmuth, ed., *Learning Disorders,* Vol. I. Seattle, Wash., Special Child Publications, 1965.

Gallagher, James J., *The Tutoring of Brain-Injured Mentally Retarded Children.* Springfield, Ill., Charles C. Thomas, 1960.

Getman, G. N., *How to Develop Your Child's Intelligence.* Luverne, Minn., the author, 1962.

Goldberg, Ilsa, "Tutoring as a Method of Psychotherapy in Schizophrenic Children with Reading Disabilities." *Quarterly Journal of Child Behavior,* 4: 273–80, 1952.

Johnson, Doris J., and Myklebust, Helmer R., *Learning Disabilities: Educational Principles and Practices.* New York, Grune & Stratton, 1967.

Kluckhohn, Clyde, *Mirror for Man.* New York, McGraw-Hill (Premier Book), 1944.

Kough, Jack, and De Haan, Robert F., *Helping Students with Special Needs.* Chicago, Science Research Associates, 1957.

Lamm, L. B., and Folsom, J. C., "Attitude Therapy and the Team Approach." *The Journal of Hospital and Community Psychiatry,* November, 1965, pp. 307–20.

Mase, Darrel J., "Emotionally Insecure and Disturbed Children," in James F. Magary and John R. Eichorn, eds., *The Exceptional Child: A Book*

Additional Aspects of the Teacher's Role

of Readings. New York, Holt, Rinehart & Winston, 1962, pp. 340–45.

Morse, William C., "The Education of Socially Maladjusted and Emotionally Disturbed Children," in William M. Cruickshank and G. Orville Johnston, eds., *Education of Exceptional Children and Youth.* Englewood Cliffs, N.J., Prentice-Hall, 1958, pp. 557–608.

New York City Board of Education, *Guidance of Children in Elementary Schools.* Curriculum Bulletin Number 13, 1955–1956 series.

Ratchik, Irving, and Koenig, Frances G., *Guidance and the Physically Handicapped Child.* Chicago, Science Research Associates, 1963.

Siegel, Ernest, *Helping the Brain Injured Child.* New York, New York Association for Brain Injured Children, 1961.

Siegel, Ernest, "Some Suggestions for Developing Effective Lessons." Mimeographed paper distributed in in-service training course, The Adams School, 248 E. 31 St., New York City, 1967.

Treatman, Paul, *Teacher's License Training Text: Assistant-to-Principal, Junior Principal, and Principal.* New York, Arco, 1957.

Wolfensberger, Wolf, "Embarrassments in the Diagnostic Process." *Mental Retardation* (published by the American Association on Mental Deficiency), Vol. 3, No. 3 (June, 1965), pp. 29–31.

Wright, Beatrice A., *Physical Disability—A Psychological Approach.* New York, Harper & Brothers, 1960.

CHAPTER

5

The Role of the School Administrator

The administrators of public school classes are generally graduates of regular teacher-training institutions. In order to establish and administer vital programs which meet the needs of the mildly handicapped child in the regular classroom, it is important that administrators undergo a special education orientation. This ongoing indoctrination can be accomplished through course work, special education literature, attendance of conferences and workshops and utilization of consultants and board of education specialists.

The net results of such training will be a greater awareness of the nature and needs of the handicapped child in the regular classroom, a consideration of modifications which can help meet these needs, an awareness of the tasks which face the classroom teacher as he endeavors to render his classroom an effective milieu for the handicapped child and support for the teacher. It can also foster a creatitive, flexible administrative approach; for example, instead of decreeing automatically that any handicapped child discovered in a regular class be transferred to a special class, the administrator will now think in terms of modifications, support and additional alternatives. Laufer (1966) cautions that a "danger of too hasty and unnecessary removal of a child from a regular to a special class . . . might be avoided by consultation and special help to the regular classroom teacher, or by providing special help outside the regular class." Shattuck (1946) reports a consensus of a group of special educators that it is best not to segregate pupils into special classes if they can receive as good—or possibly even better—education in the regular grades, *although it may necessitate special help.*

Perhaps the overall ingredient is acceptance. The handicapped child in the regular classroom requires the acceptance of the school principal, the teacher and his peers (Arnold 1966). These are intertwined and are mutually dependent: The likelihood that the classroom teacher will accept the handicapped child is very much related to the accepting attitude of the administrator.

The administrator must support his teachers in a variety of ways: in-service training, appropriate materials, provision for parent conferences, resource personnel and ancillary services, etc. Moreover, the teachers must receive approval and encouragement when they refer learning and behavioral problems for review and observation (Bowden and Otto 1964: 155). Their opinions should not be taken lightly, nor should the administrator construe these referrals as reflecting the teacher's inadequacies or a shirking attitude. Young (1967: 134) states that many learning problems "can be handled in the regular classroom by giving some assistance either to the teacher or to the child and by reducing the number of children in the class."

The enlightened administrator always considers the child— especially the child with special needs—to be the ultimate beneficiary of all administrative measures. However, for purposes of grouping, the focus of concern falls broadly into three categories: the teacher, the child and the program.

Supporting the Teacher

The in-service training needs of regular classroom teacher can be met by in-service courses (preferably conducted in or near the school to eliminate excessive traveling after the teaching day), university courses and institutes (the administrator may be helpful in bringing these to the teacher's attention and possibly assist in course selection), workshops and demonstration courses. Financial and promotional incentives are useful, and the administrator may be instrumental in effecting such policies. Consultants (board of education personnel or private specialists) are often readily available training resources. Many school systems employ an itinerant special education teacher. In addition to offering occasional individual instruction to the handicapped child, the itinerant teacher's major role regarding the mildly handicapped child in the regular classroom is to offer teaching suggestions to the regular teacher. In addition, teacher competency and professional growth are often enhanced through such techniques and services as intervisitations, professional school libraries, exhibits and bulletins, observations and even plan book inspection. Staff conferences are particularly important in that the teacher may be able to explore questions directly related to the handicapped children in his classroom.

The administrator should provide the classroom teacher with measures that are basically "relief" in nature. Small class size is an important factor since it permits the teacher to devote more of his time and efforts toward helping the child with special needs. Teaching assistants and relief from excessive clerical chores are additional means of freeing the teacher. A relatively new concept is the "crisis teacher" (Morse 1965); the emotionally disturbed child in the regular classroom, when it is the opinion of his teacher that he can't be helped in the classroom alone, is referred to the crisis teacher, who is situated in a different room. Pupils may visit the crisis teacher episodically or on an ongoing basis, but still spend the majority of time with the regular classroom teacher. In addition to working with behavior problems, the crisis teachers can, when time permits, render individual help to underachieving children.

In addition, the administrator provides vital supervision and makes constructive criticism, conducting democratic teacher-supervisor (or principal) conferences. He recognizes signs of growth and praises the teacher's accomplishments. He recognizes that the teacher is on the firing line, that his job is demanding, exacting and difficult; he is aware of his dedication and talent. All of this is conveyed to the teacher, the parents, other professionals and to the community.

The subject of teacher competency is intimately linked with the topic of teacher recruitment and selection: That is to say, input (the kind of teacher initially employed) certainly influences output (quality of teacher performance). It is desirable for the school administrator to evaluate the training and experience of the prospective teacher, to conduct interviews and to explain the nature of the pending assignment, pointing out the responsibilities entailed in helping the handicapped child in the regular classroom (Bowden and Otto 1964: 126). It has been pointed out (Voelker 1958: 658) that the successful teacher of special education classes must possess certain qualities, among which are: (1) high intelligence, (2) strong social feeling, (3) warm and friendly personality, (4) sincere interest in handicapped children, (5) technical skills in working in specific area of specialization (deaf, orthopedically handicapped, mentally retarded, etc.) and (6) ability to adjust well in the school and community. The public school administrator seeking regular teachers might use these very guidelines (with the possible exception of number 5, substituting for technical skills in a specific area of specialization a strong foundation in child development and/or mental hygiene course work). Since the law of supply and demand is a constant factor, it may very well be that an administrator at times will have to select a less qualified teacher, but one who evidences potential—an open mind coupled with the ability and *willingness* to grow, both professionally and technically.

The administrator must be active in teacher recruitment, seeking to stimulate interest in potential teachers from various sources, including high school students, young college students and older women who, having resigned to raise a family, may now wish to return to teaching (Voelker 1958: 657). Some schools have career guidance programs even on the junior high school level. Enthusiasm is contagious; the public school administrator, committed to help the handicapped child in the regular classroom, is often able to influence prospective teachers toward this challenging and necessary goal.

Supporting the Child

The administrator can help the child by developing and utilizing adjunct pupil personnel services such as attendance bureaus, guidance bureaus, speech departments, health education bureaus, etc. These services can have direct bearing upon the learning and/or behaviorally impaired children in the regular classroom. For example, some stated goals of the Bureau of Attendance of New York City Board of Education (Division of Child Welfare 1960–1961) are to "prevent unnecessary absences, identify causative factors, and develop positive interpersonal relationships which will motivate maladjusted children toward better attendance habits. . . ." In the same vein, the health education bureau can make a major thrust toward suggesting modifications in the gym programs which will be feasible to carry out in regular gym periods, yet be of special benefit to the minimally brain-injured child.

The handicapped child in the regular classroom may require the intervention of ancillary services. These include counseling (possibly psychotherapy), other therapies (speech, occupational, physiotherapy), visual training and individual remediation (reading, arithmetic, etc.). These are sometimes available in the school building; in other instances, the child must go elsewhere for these ancillary services. The administrator utilizes them (helping to establish them when necessary) and works cooperatively with them. Referring a child to these services, particularly tutoring, is not a reflection of the school program's inadequacies but signifies an adherence to the concept of the whole child and a recognition of individual differences.

A definitive school guidance policy is needed. All too often, even when guidance counselors are employed in the school, the child with mild learning and/or behavioral problems is often overlooked. Krugman (1954: 115) pointed out that since school guidance programs are invariably understaffed, there is a tendency to focus on only the "emergency" problems (*e.g.*, the acting-out child). Certainly then, the needs of the learning and/or behaviorally impaired children, even the mild "ignorable" ones, at least on a preventative basis, can require the intervention of guidance personnel. Very often, despite the existence of written school records denoting a specific psychologically or medically handicapping condition, these records are simply ignored. Teachers fail to read them; guidance counselors (or school psychologists) do not interpret them to teachers; neither case conferences nor staff conferences concerning the children are conducted. Especially in the upper grades, in a departmentalized program, the mildly handicapped child in the regular classroom can best be served if his various teachers learn about the nature and needs of his condition. Parents are frequently placed in a position of (1) having to inform teachers of the child's medical or psychological condition—and of the existence of the school folder—and (2) suggesting some ameliorative measures. Clearly, this situation places teachers on the defensive. It would be more judicious for the school administrator to effect such procedures as case conferences, guidance counselor-teacher consultation, etc. There is a paradox concerning the child's confidential folder. Parents often inquire of professionals, "Should I tell the school of my child's diagnosis and problems? Is it wise to get all of this on his record?" In reality, the parents' real problem is not the dilemma of whether or not to initiate a "record," but to get the school personnel to look at it and do something about it! It is unfortunate that dedicated school personnel find themselves unable to achieve the favorable results they seek because of such factors as large classes, insufficient guidance staff and lack of special provision for the increasing numbers of disruptive children found in regular classes.

In considering the purely administrative routine aspects of a definitive guidance policy (record keeping and *sharing*, establishment of case conferences, provision for *ongoing* meetings between guidance counselor and teacher as well as between guidance counselor and child, etc.), there are some overall tenets of school guidance—pertinent to all children, but of special significance to the mildly handicapped child in the regular classroom. The Board of Education of the City of New York (1955–1966: 2–6) lists the following basic concepts underlying a public school guidance program:*

1. Guidance includes personal and social as well as educational and vocational areas.
2. Guidance must be related to a functional curriculum to meet children's needs.
3. The guidance point of view must pervade the thinking of the personnel of the school: attitude toward children, emphasis on growth and development, development of mental health concept.
4. Sound guidance is based upon knowledge of children and an interest in learning about them.
5. Guidance is based on the recognition of the child as an individual.
6. Guidance takes into consideration the emotional needs of children and, as far as possible, implements these needs.
7. Guidance is inseparable from teaching.
8. No single technique of guidance is effective under all conditions.
9. Guidance is concerned with causes as well as symptoms.
10. Development problems are normal.

* Reprinted from Curriculum Bulletin 1955–1956 of the Board of Education entitled "Guidance of Children in the Elementary School," by permission of the Board of Education of the City of New York.

11. Guidance, to be successful, must have direction by the head of the school.

The school administrator can support the handicapped child in the regular classroom by instilling in the teacher "the guidance point of view." Chamberlain and Kindred (1958: 330–1) believe that there is no "forbidden ground" which divides the teacher's instruction and guidance responsibilities, but that the teacher's "greatest [guidance] contribution lies in the direction and control of the instructional process. He can adjust learning activities to differences found among pupils. . . ."

Finally, the child is bolstered to the extent that the school administrator succeeds in setting up positive lines of communication with the parent. Inasmuch as parent attitudes and anxieties are invariably transmitted to the child, it is vital that the parent and school work harmoniously toward mutually approved, realistic yet optimistic goals. A school program in which the parent is considered an essential factor would include parent orientation utilizing such techniques as frequently issued newsletters, parent conferences, parent-teacher meetings, participation in PTA activities, parent observation of classrooms and group meetings of parents of similarly handicapped children (Bowden and Otto 1964: 131). In addition to parent orientation, the administrator must provide the opportunity for the teacher and other personnel to communicate with the parent; the converse—*i.e.,* the machinery whereby the parent can initiate the conference—is equally important. The school may be instrumental in providing parent counseling, or at least in making a referral for such service. All children are affected by the attitudes of their parents. In the case of learning and/or behavioral problems, because of paucity of meaningful peer relationships and experiences, the child is even more emotionally dependent upon his parents for feedback, attitudes and values; hence, the importance of working for the child *through* the parent.

The school administrator can further serve the child by setting up ongoing screening and placement policies. He should establish a hierarchal range of placement possibilities for handicapped children: regular (or even gifted) class placement with no administrative modification, regular class with an itinerant teacher as consultant, regular class in conjunction with a resource room and specialist (*e.g.,* "sight conservation" cases), part special and part regular classes, or special class placement on a full-time basis. The placement policy should be ongoing, subject to frequent review, rather than irrevocable.

Even retention is a bona fide placement possibility. In all instances, the "on trial" aspect should be conveyed to the parents. If it becomes necessary, in the view of those making the placement decisions, to retain a child, to place him on home instruction, to put him in a "slower" class or to transfer him from a regular class to a special class setting, the parents must be made to feel that there will be continual observation and evaluation, and should the necessary improvement or adjustment occur, reassignment to a regular class will ensue.

Supporting the Program

The administrator must make appropriate teaching materials available to the classroom teacher. He must keep abreast of current developments in special education materials, equipment and programs. Many of the materials, though primarily created for exceptional children, often have considerable merit for all children. Some examples of such materials are the Frostig Program for the Development of Visual Perception, Stern's Structural Arithmetic, Cuisinaire Rods, the Turner-Livingston Communication Series, the Illinois Test for Psycholinguistic Abilities, Peabody Language Development Kits, the Continental Press workbooks, Teaching Resources (an educational service of the New York *Times*), Montessori materials, etc. In addition, the administrator must take into account the need for texts that portray minority races—particularly Negroes—in a favorable light (Larrick 1965). For years, our school books, including periodicals, children's literature and social studies texts, have omitted the Negro from historical accounts, poked fun at him, alluded to his "innate" inferiority, portrayed him as the "natural" personal servant of the white man and in general depicted him as somewhat subhuman (Millender 1966). Such constant and unrelenting bigotry, in its printed form in school texts approved by boards of education, *seems* to bear a certain aura of truth. Certainly there is a direct relationship between the existence of such literature and the development of deepseated feelings of low self-esteem, which, in turn, can result in learning and behavioral problems. Fortunately, there have been some inroads toward eliminating such prejudicial propaganda from teaching materials (for example, the Bank Street Readers).

The administrator can make specific program modifications, almost mechanical in nature, that can enable the mildly handicapped child to participate successfully in the regular classroom program. The following are some examples:

1. Occasionally, it may be desirable for a child to be permitted to arrive a few minutes later and leave a few minutes earlier than the rest of the class, thereby avoiding the crowds of arriving and departing children. (This could be a worthwhile practice in the case of some overly shy children; similarly, a brain-injured child may be overwhelmed or overly excited by large groups of children.)

2. A disorganized child may benefit by being permitted to have a double set of school books—one set for home, and the other to remain in school. This eliminates the need for carrying books to school.

3. An easily available duplicating machine enables the teacher to prepare work sheets, printed instructions, homework assignments, examinations, etc., substantially reducing the amount of blackboard copying normally done. Children who

have difficulty in visual-motor coordination will benefit greatly by this.

4. Apprising out-of-class personnel such as bus drivers or the lunch-room aide of the nature of a particular child's problems may suggest a specific modification (a seat nearer the bus driver, subtle assistance in carrying a tray of food, etc.).

5. A school phobic may have to be eased into the school program. He may have to attend school for brief periods at first, and gradually increase the length of attendance. Initially, his mother may have to accompany him and stay with him, then make the separation gradually. At first, the child may have to spend some time in a room such as the principal's office or the guidance counselor's office before attending the classroom.

6. Extracurricular activities could be created at times, geared toward helping the marginally handicapped child who has special needs. The child, in turn, could be guided toward participating in these. Arts and crafts or athletics can be helpful for children with coordination problems. Debating clubs or drama groups can help children who have communication problems. Chess and checkers can help children who need to develop socialization skills but are ready only for one-to-one, rather than group, experiences.

An important aspect of the overall program is evaluation. The administrator must devise means of judging the efficacy of the material, the program, the curriculum. There are many evaluative instruments; observation should not be the sole technique. The opinions of the teachers, the parents and the children themselves can be extremely valuable.

Evaluation includes a longitudinal aspect; an effective articulation must be established with "feeding" schools. For example, the junior high school administrator should confer with his counterpart in the source elementary school, suggesting specific means by which the elementary school might better prepare the mildly handicapped child for the junior high school program.

Similarly, the high school administrator must work closely with vocational counselors, rehabilitation agencies and college personnel. By "zeroing in" on the requirements of the future, the administrator can effect current curricular changes.

Working with the Community

The child is a member of a community. Lines of force flow in two directions: from the child to the community and from the community to the child. The school administrator, who endeavors to help the handicapped child in the regular classroom must consider the various community vectors that relate to the handicapped: the negative forces (problems, prejudices, lack of opportunity) as well as the positive ones (physical resources, employment possibilities, growing public concern for children with special needs, funds and resource personnel).

The community can often be called upon to assist a special aspect of a school program (a visual training program, modified athletics and the like) by donating funds, equipment or volunteer professional personnel. Professionals within the community can address assemblies of students, assist in career guidance and orient groups of parents. Businessmen may offer vocational training and/or employment to the mildly handicapped within the community. There is a dearth of after-school (afternoon, weekend, summer) social-recreational groups for the minimally handicapped. The ones that exist for the more severely handicapped child do not meet the needs of the mildly handicapped child and may even be harmful to him. Similarly, he generally meets rejection in those settings that are geared solely to the normal child. To help establish social-recreational facilities for the mildly handicapped, the school administrator may work directly with local churches, civic groups and businessmen.

Other professional institutions within the community can become more aware of the unique problems of the mildly handicapped child—particularly the learning and/or behavioral problems—and may, upon the school administrator's advice, gear portions of their programs more toward these children. These institutions include mental health clinics, medical diagnostic centers, speech and hearing units, educational clinics, etc.

The school administrator can become active with parent groups (*i.e.*, parents of handicapped children) within the community. He can draw upon the community for teacher recruitment. He may even wish to advise the local libraries of pertinent books and periodicals—reading materials that might lead to greater public acceptance of the handicapped.

Although there has been some improvement in the fate of the handicapped at the hands of the community (better institutional care, child labor laws, mandated jurisdiction of juvenile courts for juvenile delinquents, establishment of welfare agencies, etc.), Kanner (1966: 262–63) cautions that the "time for rejoicing is still far off. Group attitudes of long standing do not change overnight." He further states that:

> *Individual pathology is closely interwoven with communal sociopathology.* Preventive mental hygiene must take this important fact into consideration. It must join hands with the forces which work for the betterment of public health, try to combat prejudices and discrimination, advocate better housing and recreational facilities. . . . Children in trouble should be a challenge to the community, not a source of negligence, ridicule, or vituperation.

The administrator can make the community more aware of the handicapped—their strengths as well as their needs—by issuing appropriate school bulletins, conducting special assembly programs and lecturing to various civic and church groups. He can encourage talented handicapped children to "perform" outside the school: city-wide spelling bees, entertaining at hospitals, school plays performed in local auditoriums, debates and leadership programs at chambers of commerce, intramural athletics, etc.

The Role of the School Administrator

In brief, the school administrator relates to the community by (1) utilizing its resources to help in the educational, social-recreational, health and vocational programs of handicapped pupils and (2) shaping the community attitude toward greater acceptance of the handicapped.

These two activities are mutually dependent, each making it possible for the administrator to achieve the ultimate goal—returning an acceptable individual to an accepting community.

In all, the administrator's job is an overwhelming one. Each child enrolled in the school is his direct responsibility. The teachers and other school personnel are directly responsible to him. He is in charge of the entire school plant. Parents will hold him responsible for the education of their children. The community will hold him accountable (morally, if not legally) for the out-of-school misconduct of his school's pupils. Administering the program entails requisitioning supplies (including storage, distribution and inventory preparation), preparing daily, monthly and annual attendance reports, recruiting, selection and training of teachers, administering health and safety measures as well as maintenance of the school building. These are only some of the administrator's functions.

How can we ask him to do even more? To stretch his imagination and his stamina so that the mildly handicapped in the regular classroom are better accommodated? The answer lies in the relegating of responsibilities. The wise administrator learns to recognize (and to nurture) the gifted teacher—the one who is able to do his job thoroughly plus "a little more." Many such teachers are both willing and able to undertake administrative chores. Care should be taken to keep these on a creative, administrative, rather than clerical, level. For example, it is more judicious to encourage a teacher to assist in evaluating and selecting a specific text, workbook or teaching aid than to ask him to prepare (in triplicate) the order list, tediously copying myriads of supply list numbers. The administrator, by so utilizing the administrative skills of the classroom teacher, not only renders his various functions more "workable," but also promotes the professional growth and positive attitude of the teacher.

REFERENCES

Arnold, Marcus, unpublished address at Center for Urban Education, New York City, June 1, 1966.

Bowden, M. G., and Otto, Henry J., *The Education of the Exceptional Child in the Casis School.* Austin, University of Texas Press, 1964.

Chamberlain, Leo M., and Kindred, Leslie W., *The Teacher and School Organization.* Englewood Cliffs, N.J., Prentice-Hall, 1958.

Division of Child Welfare, Board of Education, City of New York, 1960–1961.

Kanner, Leo, *Child Psychiatry,* Springfield, Ill., Charles C. Thomas, 1966.

Krugman, Morris, "Appraisal and Treatment of Personality Problems in a Guidance Program," in *Education in a Free World.* Washington, D.C., American Council on Education, 1954, pp. 114–21.

Laufer, Maurice, "Emotionally Disturbed and Brain-Injured Children's Problems of Education." *Canada's Mental Health,* Vol. 14, No. 4 (1966), pp. 21–23.

Larrick, Nancy, "The All-White World of Children Books." *Saturday Review,* September 11, 1965.

Millender, Dharatula, M., "Selecting Our Children's Books: Time for Some Changes." *Changing Education: A Journal of the American Federation of Teachers,* Fall, 1966, pp. 8–14.

Morse, William C., "The Crisis Teacher" in Nicholas J. Long, William C. Morse, and Ruth G. Newman, eds., *Conflict in the Classroom.* Belmont, Calif., Wadsworth, 1966, pp. 251–54.

New York City Board of Education, *Guidance of Children in Elementary Schools.* Curriculum Bulletin, Number 13, 1955–1956 series.

Shattuck, Marquis, "Segregation versus Non-Segregation of Exceptional Children." *Journal of Exceptional Children,* 12: 235–40 (May, 1946).

Voelker, Paul H., "Administration and Supervision of Special Education Programs," in William M. Cruickshank and G. Orville Johnson, eds., *Education of Exceptional Children and Youth.* Englewood Cliffs, N.J., Prentice-Hall, 1958, pp. 648–98.

Young, Milton A., *Teaching Children with Special Learning Needs: A Problem-Solving Approach.* New York, John Day, 1967.

CHAPTER

6

The Role of Teacher-Training Institutions

Teachers of regular classes and their school administrators are, for the most part, products of a general education training. Handicapped children, particularly the mildly handicapped, are found in greater prevalence in regular classes than in special classes. Hence it behooves teacher-training institutions to examine their programs from the viewpoint of meeting the needs of the mildly handicapped child enrolled in the regular classroom. Are the concepts and bodies of knowledge encountered in general education teacher-training programs adequate (*i.e.,* providing sufficient specifics) in preparing teachers to work with the exceptional child? Can a broadening of philosophical goals, perhaps a shift in emphasis, result in greater teacher competency? In this vein, the major roles for teacher-training institutions are (1) teacher preparation (including teacher selection and teacher guidance), (2) working with the community and (3) research.

Teacher Preparation

The greatest modification that can be made and should be made is the inclusion of some specific special education course work for *all* teachers. There is a trend toward this; some universities now offer an Introduction to Special Education in the general education sequence. (Unfortunately, however, in many cases, this is elective rather than required). This course should be offered on an undergraduate level as well as on a graduate level so that prospective elementary teachers, pursuing their B.A. degrees in education, can become oriented to the exceptional child—a child they are statistically likely to meet in their classrooms. Traditionally, special education courses have been offered on the graduate rather than on the undergraduate level. This was so largely because it was felt that the best teachers of special education are those who have first demonstrated successful teaching experience with normal classes. In fact, the very nomenclature lends itself to this belief: Does not the word "special" in "special education" have a general, plus "something else" connotation? The trend, however, is changing. In discussing teacher preparation for the emotionally disturbed, Johnson (1968: 347, 351) cites research to show that "longer training does not necessarily mean better training" and that lack of teaching experience "does not seem to be a drawback in preparing undergraduates. Given the choice between teaching experience and openness to change (flexibility), potential for change should take precedence."

Secondary school teachers are often thought to be, by training if not by inclination, "subject oriented" rather than "child oriented." Normal children, possessing greater inner resources (psychological as well as educational) than the exceptional— even the marginally exceptional—child, need not be significantly handicapped by this circumstance. However, the needs of the learning and/or behaviorally impaired child in the regular classroom might be more fully met if the secondary teacher's training included more child development and methodology studies as well as some special education course work.

The special education course should have a great deal of practical emphasis—stressing methods, observation and demonstration, even some student teaching. Frequently authorities say that experience in teaching *handicapped* children often increases the competencies of teachers of *regular* children. The National Society for the Study of Education (1950: 5-6) states that "the methods which have been developed for exceptional children have yielded gratifying results in the education of other children. . . . We learn about the 'normal' from the 'abnormal.' Many educational practices for the correction of social maladjustments have proved to be excellent preventative methods for all. . . . The activity movement . . . in which it was emphasized that the mentally defective could learn best . . . [by *"doing"*] was later advocated as a general educational procedure. . . ."

A teacher of a blind child in a regular classroom reported that she gained "a renewed sensitivity to individual differences, a greater appreciation of the exceptional child, an expansion of patience, a growth in adaptability and development of confidence" (Waleski 1964: 13). Waleski (1964: 14) also presents the case of a teacher who worked with a hard-of-hearing child in a regular classroom. The proper functioning of the child's hearing aid demanded a decrease of excess noise. The resulting quiet (less scraping of chairs, slamming of books and doors, etc.) helped everyone, particularly the "normal" student with a poor attention span. Waleski concludes that—"the classroom experience with these children provides a learning laboratory for teaching all children" and—perhaps the crux of the exceptional child-normal child relationship—"teachers confronted by special needs are forced to analyze their teaching methods." This concept of "necessity being the mother of invention" (the confrontation of a handicapped child by a regular classroom teacher *forces* the teacher to analyze the learning and teaching process) is further amplified by Johnson and Myklebust (1967, Preface). Underlying the objective of their book *Learning Disabilities,* which focuses entirely upon children who present disorders in learning that stem from psychoneurological factors, is "the hope that the concepts and materials might be a contribution to better understanding of learning as a process and thereby enhance this vital experience for all children."

Parallel to the need for special education courses is the need for basic child development courses. Often the handicapped can be understood only through a basic knowledge of normal child development—for example, the mental retardate's mental age is that of a younger, normal child; many of the behavior traits of minimally brain-injured children are similar to the normal behavior of younger children; the emotionally disturbed child is often emotionally and socially *immature*. In discussing disturbed children, Walsh and O'Connor (1968: 354) believe that "a basic aspect of the teacher's role in prevention is the ability to distinguish between behavior that indicates emotional malfunctioning and behavior that is normal and developmentally appropriate for school-age children of a certain age, sex, culture, and grade."

In addition, it is recommended that teacher-training programs, both in general education and special education sequences, include some experience in teaching on a one-to-one basis. In teaching individually, the teacher becomes skilled in defining the specific aim, in developing a logical sequence of activities and in adaptability (*i.e.,* if the one child he is teaching doesn't grasp the idea, the teacher is forced to rephrase, to employ an alternate method, to emphasize a different sense modality, etc.). Furthermore, the instant evaluation inherent in individual instruction permits a degree of refinement (*i.e.,* keeping those methods and materials that work, but changing those that are ineffective) not to be found in teaching groups of children. Teachers who have worked with groups of children as well as with individual pupils often remark that the experience gained in teaching one child individually enhances their skill in working with groups of children by promoting greater awareness of individual differences, a finer understanding of the learning as well as the teaching process, a better understanding of, and the ability to deal with such problems as lack of motivation, poor work habits, distractibility, etc.

Often, the university, in an effort to create a more positive image of itself or to insure a higher accreditation, may, ironically, find itself establishing policies that militate against the ultimate goal—teacher preparation. Some examples are:
1. The practice of employing only full-time, rather than some part-time college instructors. Many of those seeking part-time college affiliations in teacher-training institutions are highly experienced in the actual process of education—they are teachers, supervisors, school principals, etc. They have had many years of successful teaching experience with children and are *currently* employed as well. Conversely, full-time college instructors often have been away from teaching children for many years. (Indeed, some never have had this experience!) Connor (1964: 208) deplores the practice of "accepting as criteria the armchair verbalizations of the inadequate but well-known expert," and points to the "theoretician with little or no knowledge of the actual teaching-learning situation." Of course, there is the practitioner who is experienced but inarticulate; hence, what is really needed is the "clinical professor, the *master teacher* with a doctorate and professional rank . . . and more *practitioners* who are scholarly and articulate" [italics added]. Many colleges do not employ part-time personnel. Even where this is done, the part-time instructors are not really welcome; this is shown by the much lower salary rate; the absence of tenure; no or insufficient office space, etc. Just as school systems often insist that principals and chairmen of departments spend some time during the day in actual classroom teaching, colleges might very well take this lead and seek—and welcome—some instructors who are *practicing* teachers. Perhaps some arrangements can be made whereby full-time professors of education are encouraged to devote some of their time to teaching children.
2. Discouragement of the part-time, commuting student. Inasmuch as most special education courses were traditionally (and even currently, though to a lesser extent) offered only on a graduate level, many students enrolling in these courses were

already teaching full-time. But colleges generally tend to favor the full-time student. Undoubtedly, this preference is rooted in the desire to encourage the enrollment of students who will be able to become completely immersed in their studies. This point is certainly well taken in that the full-time students have more time to devote to any given course, can take a substantial number of courses at once rather than chip away spasmodically at degree requirements, are available for enrichment activities such as field trips and noncredit seminars, and have more opportunities to arrange conferences with their professors. The advantages of pursuing studies on a full-time basis are self-evident; nevertheless, the part-time working students often feel (whether justifiably or not) that they are being contrasted unfavorably to the full-time resident student, that they are looked upon with a certain degree of disdain, and that their dedication is in question since they have not made the sacrifices necessary to enroll full-time. This feeling of partiality may be further conveyed to them by: (a) an inordinate work load (term papers, readings, field visits, etc.) often impossible to satisfy if one is teaching full-time, (b) scheduling of important courses earlier than 3 P.M., (c) the "overnight reserve" borrowing policy for many college library reference books, and (d) the reluctance of some college instructors to utilize the part-time students' teaching experience as a class resource.

Another important aspect of teacher preparation is the area of teacher selection. Some guidelines should be drawn up by which those obviously unfit for teaching are discouraged from becoming education majors. Certainly such factors as intelligence, scholarship, personality and emotional stability should be considered. In projecting ahead, envisioning the prospective teacher in the regular classroom, the professor of education should consider not only the normal children, but the handicapped as well. For example, it is believed (U.S. Office of Education 1957: 10–17) that the teacher of emotionally disturbed children should: (1) understand child growth and development in addition to the nature and needs of the emotionally disturbed; (2) understand the nature of learning problems; (3) be aware of social and cultural factors; (4) have a knowledge of the relevant community agencies; (5) have insight into herself and be aware of her own limitations, and (6) be able to work with parents without becoming emotionally involved.

Some other requirements (or rules) for the effective teacher of the emotionally disturbed are thought to be objectivity, flexibility, structure, social reinforcement, curricular expertise and intellectual model (Hewett 1966). Cheyney (1966: 87) believes that the most important quality for teachers of the culturally disadvantaged is respect for the pupil.

A concomitant of teacher selection and teacher preparation is guidance and counseling. A well-rounded teacher-training institution will make provisions for these. Hewett (1966: 8) believes that the competent teacher "has some recognition of his own emotional needs and attempts to separate these from the needs of his students."

Working with the Community

Teacher-training institutions can help the mildly handicapped child in the regular classroom by working closely with the community. Laboratory schools, education clinics, speech clinics, demonstration courses and other such projects train teachers while simultaneously servicing children. Some universities have offered campus space and equipment for community social-recreational programs involving handicapped children. Volunteers to man these programs can be recruited from education courses, such assignments often being the basis for term projects.

Education departments can further serve the handicapped in the community by providing speakers and consultants. Such resource people can participate at church groups, civic and fraternal associations, parent groups, etc.

Teacher-training personnel can play a vital role in guiding parent organizations. Voelker (1958: 681–82) points out that: "These groups, composed of parents of handicapped children, offer a haven of mutual understanding not available from any other source. Because they share similar problems, the parent members are able to gain insight not possible through other experience. When provided with wise leadership, these organizations can be powerful agents for the betterment of exceptional children. . . ."

Through workshops, conferences and conventions, often in co-sponsorship with state departments of education, local boards of education, other city and state agencies such as departments of health, mental health bureaus, etc., and parent groups, the universities can focus attention on the handicapped. By participation in such programs, the academic community as well as the community at large becomes more cognizant of the handicapped and of their respective roles in helping them meet their needs.

Research

The rate of research in the behavioral sciences over the past five years has been extremely accelerated. Some of the reasons for this are (1) an increased interest in the study of behavior, (2) recent findings in medicine, chemistry, psychology and sociology, (3) refinement of research techniques and instruments (statistical methods, data processing, computers, etc.), (4) the existence of hitherto unavailable funds earmarked for research purposes, and (5) increase in graduate school enrollment, research being one of the prime requirements for the doctoral degree.

This emphasis upon research brings funds, staff, prestige and talented students to the universities. Thus, teacher-training institutions can help the handicapped child in the regular classroom by conducting appropriate research projects such as prevalent studies (these can help discover the mildly handicapped and at the same time create an instrument of detection—*e.g.*, a checklist—by which the classroom teacher initiates identification) ; longitudinal studies (these answer the question "What happens to these children as they grow older?" thereby enabling us to formulate and refine their educational experiences) ; attitude studies (parents, teachers, children) ; evaluation of materials, methods, screening and placement practices; "cluster" studies (examining correlations of environmental and genetic factors in relation to a specific category of exceptionality to see if a particular psychological/medical diagnostic entity correlates with a pattern—*i.e.*, a cluster of causal factors) , etc.

Clearly, the findings of such research projects can redound to the benefit of the handicapped pupils. In addition, the teacher-training institution can instill the "research" point of view in its students, thereby promoting inquiry, even self-examination where needed, willingness to consider another point of view, the ability to evaluate and research consumer skills.

REFERENCES

Cheyney, Arnold B., "Teachers of the Culturally Disadvantaged." *Exceptional Children,* 33: 2 (October, 1966) , pp. 83–88.

Connor, Frances P., "Excellence in Special Education." *Exceptional Children,* Vol. 30, No. 5 (January, 1964) , pp. 206–9.

Hewett, Frank M., "A Hierarchy of Competencies for Teachers of Emotionally Handicapped Children." *Exceptional Children,* Vol. 33, No. 1 (September, 1966) , pp. 7–11.

Johnson, Doris J., and Myklebust, Helmer R., *Learning Disabilities: Educational Principles and Practices.* New York, Grune & Stratton, 1967.

Johnson, John L., "Teacher Preparation for Educating the Disturbed: Graduate, Undergraduate, or Functional?" *Exceptional Children,* Vol. 34, No. 5 (January, 1968) , pp. 345–51.

National Society for the Study of Education, *Forty Ninth Yearbook,* Part II. Chicago, University of Chicago Press, 1950.

U.S. Office of Education Bulletin No. 11, "Teachers of Children Who Are Socially and Emotionally Maladjusted," prepared by Romain Mackie, William C. Kvaraceus, and Harold Williams, 1957.

Voelker, Paul H., "Administration and Supervision of Special Education Programs," in William M. Cruickshank and G. Orville Johnson, eds., *Education of Exceptional Children and Youth*. Englewood Cliffs, N.J., Prentice-Hall, 1958, pp. 648–98.

Waleski, Dorothy, "The Physically Handicapped in the Classroom." *NEA Journal*, Vol. 53, No. 9 (December, 1964), pp. 12–16.

Walsh, John F., and O'Connor, Sister James Dolores, "When Are Children Disturbed?" *The Elementary School Journal*, April, 1968, pp. 353–56.

Bibliography

Arnold, Marcus, unpublished address at Center for Urban Education, New York City held on June 1, 1966.
Baker, Harry J., *Introduction to Special Education,* New York, Macmillan, 1959.
Baldwin, Willie Kate, "The Educable Mentally Retarded Child in the Regular Grades." *Exceptional Children,* 25: 106–108, 112 (November, 1958).
Barsch, Ray H., "Six Factors in Learning," in Jerome Hellmuth, ed., *Learning Disorders,* Vol. I. Seattle, Wash., Special Child Publications, Seattle Sequin School, 1965, pp. 329–43.
Beck, Harry S., "Detecting Psychological Symptoms of Brain-Injury." *Exceptional Children,* 28: 57–62 (September, 1961).
Bender, Lauretta, "Childhood Schizophrenia." *Psychiatric Quarterly,* 27: 663–681, 1953.
Black, Millard H., "Characteristics of the Culturally Disadvantaged Child," in Joe L. Frost and Glenn R. Hawkes, eds., *The Disadvantaged Child.* Boston, Houghton Mifflin, 1966, pp. 45–50.
Blackham, Garth J., *The Deviant Child in the Classroom.* Belmont, Calif., Wadsworth, 1967.
Blackman, Leonard S., "The Brave New World of Special Education." Teachers College, Columbia University, N.P., n.d.
Blackman, Leonard S., and Sparks, Howard L., "What Is Special about Special Education Revisited: The Mentally Retarded." *Exceptional Children,* 31: 242–47 (January, 1965).
Blatt, Burton, "Some Persistently Recurring Assumptions Concerning the Mentally Retarded." *Training School Bulletin,* 57: 48–59 (August, 1960).
Bowden, M. G., and Otto, Henry J., *The Education of the Exceptional Child in Casis School.* Austin, University of Texas Press, 1964.
Bower, Eli M., and Lambert, Nadine M., "In-School Screening of Children with Emotional Handicaps," in Nicholas J. Long, William C. Morse, and Ruth G. Newman, eds., *Conflict in the Classroom.* Belmont, Calif., Wadsworth, 1966, pp. 128–34.
Bower, Eli M., "Comparison of the Characteristics of Identified Emotionally Disturbed Children with Other Children in Classes," in E. Philip Trapp and Philip Himelstein, eds., *Readings on the Exceptional Child.* New York, Appleton-Century-Crofts, 1962, pp. 610–28.
Bower, Eli M., "Emotionally Handicapped Child and the School." *Exceptional Children,* 26: 233–42 (January, 1960).
Bower, Eli M., "A Process for Identifying Disturbed Children." *Children,* 4: 143–47 (July, 1957).
Bradley, Charles, "Organic Factors in the Psychopathology of Childhood,"

in Paul H. Hoch and Joseph Zubin, eds., *Psychopathology of Childhood*. New York, Grune & Stratton, 1955, pp. 82–104.

Chamberlain, Leo M., and Kindred, Leslie W., *The Teacher and School Organization*. Englewood Cliffs, N.J., Prentice-Hall, 1958.

Cheyney, Arnold B., "Teachers of the Culturally Disadvantaged." *Exceptional Children*, 33: 2 (October, 1966), pp. 83–88.

Child, Irvin L., and Bacon, Margaret K., "Cultural Pressures and Achievement Motivation," in Paul H. Hoch and Joseph Zubin, eds., *Psychopathology of Childhood*. New York, Grune & Stratton, 1955.

Clark, Kenneth, "Rejected Minority Group Children," in James F. Magary and John R. Eichorn, eds., *The Exceptional Child: A Book of Readings*. New York, Holt, Rinehart & Winston, 1962, pp. 460–65.

Clements, Sam D., *Minimal Brain Dysfunction in Children: Terminology and Identification*. (Phase one of a three-phase project), National Institute of Neurological Diseases and Blindness Monograph No. 3. Washington, D.C., U.S. Department of Health, Education and Welfare, 1966.

Cohn, Robert, and Nardini, John E., "The Correlation of Bilateral Occipital Slow Activity in the Human E.E.G. with Certain Disorders of Behavior." *American Journal of Psychiatry*, 115: 44–54, 1958.

Connor, Frances P., "Excellence in Special Education." *Exceptional Children*, Vol. 30, No. 5 (January, 1964), pp. 206–9.

Connor, Frances P., "The Education of Crippled Children," in William M. Cruickshank and G. Orville Johnson, eds., *Education of Exceptional Children and Youth*. Englewood Cliffs, N.J., Prentice-Hall, 1958, pp. 429–97.

Conrad, Earl, *The Public School Scandal*. New York, John Day, 1951.

Cruickshank, William M., *The Brain-Injured Child in Home, School, and Community*. Syracuse, N.Y., Syracuse University Press, 1967.

Cruickshank, William M., Bentzen, Florence A., Ratzeburg, Frederick H., and Tannhauser, Mirian F., *A Teaching Method for Brain-Injured and Hyperactive Children*. Syracuse, N.Y., Syracuse University Press, 1961.

Cruickshank, William M., "The Exceptional Child in the Elementary and Secondary Schools," in William M. Cruickshank and G. Orville Johnson, eds., *Education of Exceptional Children and Youth*. Englewood Cliffs, N.J., Prentice-Hall, 1958.

Cruickshank, William M., "The Development of Education for Exceptional Children," in William M. Cruickshank and G. Orville Johnson, eds., *Education of Exceptional Children and Youth*. Englewood Cliffs, N.J., Prentice-Hall, 1958.

Division of Child Welfare, Board of Education, City of New York, 1960–1961.

Dolch, Edward William, *Helping Handicapped Children in School*. Champaign, Ill., Garrard Press, 1948.

Doll, Edgar A., "The Essentials of an Inclusive Concept of Mental Deficiency." *American Journal on Mental Deficiency*, Vol. 46, No. 2 (October, 1941), pp. 214–19.

Doll, Edgar A., *Behavior Syndromes of CNS Impairment*. A Devereaux Reprint. Devon, Pa., Devereaux Schools, n.d.

Dunn, Lloyd M., *Exceptional Children in the Schools*. New York, Holt, Rinehart & Winston, 1963.

Dunsing, Jack D., and Kephart, Newell C., "Motor Generalizations in Space and Time," in Jerome Hellmuth, ed., *Learning Disorders*, Vol. I. Seattle, Wash., Seattle Sequin School, Special Child Publications, 1965.

Eisenberg, Leon, "School Phobia: A Study in the Communication of Anxiety," in E. Philip Trapp and Philip Himelstein, eds., *Readings on the Exceptional Child*. New York, Appleton-Century-Crofts, 1962, pp. 629–39.

Enstrom, E. A., "Handwriting for the Retarded: Out of the Classroom." *Exceptional Children*, 32: 385–88 (February, 1966).

Epps, Helen O., McCammon, Gertrude B., and Simmons, Queen O., *Teaching Devices for Children with Impaired Learning*. Columbus, Ohio, The Parents' Volunteer Association-Columbus State School, 1958.

Fine, Marvin J., "Attitudes of Regular and Special Teachers Toward the Educable Mentally Retarded Child." *Exceptional Children*, Vol. 33, No. 6 (February, 1967), pp. 429–30.

Freedman, Sanford J., Grunebaum, Henry U., and Greenblatt, Milton, "Perceptive and Cognitive Changes in Sensory Deprivation," in Philip Solomon, et al., eds., *Sensory Deprivation: A Symposium Held at Harvard Medical School*. Cambridge, Mass., Harvard University Press, 1961.

Freidus, Elizabeth, "New Approaches in Special Education of the Brain-Injured Child," in *The "Brain-Injured" Child*. New York, New York Association for Brain Injured Children, n.d., pp. 14–18.

Fremont, Herbert, "Some Thoughts on Teaching Mathematics to Disadvantaged Groups," in Joe L. Frost and Glenn R. Hawkes, eds., *The Disadvantaged Child*. Boston, Houghton Mifflin, 1966, pp. 316–23.

Frost, Joe L., and Hawkes, Glenn R., "The Disadvantaged Child: Overview and Recommendations," in *The Disadvantaged Child*. Boston, Houghton Mifflin, 1966.

Frostig, Marianne, and Horne, David, "An Approach to the Treatment of Children with Learning Disorders," in Jerome Hellmuth, ed., *Learning Disorders*, Vol. I. Seattle, Wash., Special Child Publications, 1965.

Frostig, Marianne, and Horne, David, "Assessment of Visual Perception and Its Importance in Education." *The A.A.M.D. Education Reporter*, 2: 11–12 (April, 1962).

Frostig, Marianne, and Horne, David, *The Frostig Program for the Development of Visual Perception: Teacher's Guide*. Chicago, Follett, 1964.

Gallagher, James J., *The Tutoring of Brain-Injured Mentally Retarded Children*. Springfield, Ill., Charles C. Thomas, 1960.

Gardner, Richard, "Psychogenic Problems of Brain-Injured Children and Their Parents." *Journal of American Academy of Child Psychiatry*, Vol. 7, No. 3 (July, 1968), pp. 471–91.

Gardner, William L., and Nisonger, Hershel W., "A Manual on Program Development in Mental Retardation." A Monograph Supplement. *American Journal of Mental Deficiency*, Vol. 66, No. 4 (January 1962).

Gesell, Arnold L., and Amatruda, Catherine S., *Developmental Diagnosis*. New York, P. B. Hoeber, 1941.

Getman, G. N., *How to Develop Your Child's Intelligence*. Luverne, Minn., the author, 1962.

Glick, Selma J., "Vocational, Educational, and Recreational Needs of the Cerebral Palsied Adult," in Samuel A. Kirk and Bluma Weiner, eds., *Behavior Research on Exceptional Children*. Washington, D.C., The Council for Exceptional Children, NEA, 1963.

Glueck, Sheldon, and Glueck, Eleanor, *Unraveling Juvenile Delinquency*. New York, The Commonwealth Fund, 1950.

Goldberg, Ilsa, "Tutoring as a Method of Psychotherapy in Schizophrenic Children with Reading Disabilities." *Quarterly Journal of Child Behavior*, 4: 273–80, 1952.

Goldfarb, William, "Effects of Early Institutional Care on Adolescent Personality: Rorschach Data." *American Journal of Orthopsychiatry*, 14: 441–47, 1944.

Goldstein, Herbert, and Seigle, Dorothy M., "Characteristics of Educable Mentally Handicapped Children," in Jerome H. Rothstein, ed., *Mental Retardation: Readings and Resources*. New York, Holt, Rinehart & Winston, 1961.

Goldstein, Kurt, and Sheerer, Martin, *Abstract and Concrete Behavior: An Experimental Study with Special Tests*. Psychological Monographs of American Psychological Associations, Vol. 53, No. 2, Washington, D.C., 1941.

Gotkin, Lassar G., "A Calendar Curriculum for Disadvantaged Kindergarten Children." *Teachers' College Record*, Vol. LXVII, No. 5 (February, 1967), pp. 406–17.

Graver, Palmer A., "Facilitating the Results of Therapy," in James F. Magary and John R. Eichorn, eds., *The Exceptional Child: A Book of Readings*. New York, Holt, Rinehart & Winston, 1962, pp. 374–80.

Gray, Doris, "The Blind Child in the Regular Classroom," in James F. Magary and John R. Eichorn, eds., *The Exceptional Child: A Book of Readings*. New York, Holt, Rinehart & Winston, 1962, pp. 258–66.

Grossman, Herbert, *Teaching the Emotionally Disturbed: A Casebook*. New York, Holt, Rinehart & Winston, 1965.

Bibliography

Hall, Calvin S., and Lindsay, Gardner, *Theories of Personality*. New York, John Wiley & Sons, 1957.
Haring, Norris G., and Whelan Richard J., "Experimental Methods in Education and Management," in Nicholas J. Long, William C. Morse, and Ruth G. Newman, eds., *Conflict in the Classroom*. Belmont, Calif., Wadsworth, 1966, pp. 389–404.
Haring, Norris G., "The Emotionally Disturbed," in Samuel Kirk and Bluma Weiner, eds., *Behavioral Research on Exceptional Children*. Washington, D.C., NEA, 1963, pp. 291–317.
Harper, Louis E., and Wright, Benjamin, "Dealing with Emotional Problems in the Classroom," in James F. Magary and John R. Eichorn, eds., *The Exceptional Child: A Book of Readings*. New York, Holt, Rinehart & Winston, 1962, pp. 354–67.
Haubrich, Vernon F., "The Culturally Disadvantaged and Teacher Education," in Joe L. Frost and Glenn R. Hawkes, eds., *The Disadvantaged Child*. Boston, Houghton Mifflin, 1966, pp. 362–68.
Havighurst, Robert J., "Who Are the Socially Disadvantaged?" in Joe L. Frost and Glenn R. Hawkes, eds., *The Disadvantaged Child*. Boston, Houghton Mifflin, 1966, pp. 15–23.
Heber, Rick, "A Manual on Terminology and Classification in Mental Retardation." Monograph Supplement to *American Journal of Mental Deficiency*, 64: 3–111 (September, 1959).
Heider, Grace M., "Adjustment Problems of the Deaf Child," in James F. Magary and John R. Eichorn, eds., *The Exceptional Child: A Book of Readings*. New York, Holt, Rinehart & Winston, 1962, pp. 304–11.
Hewett, Frank M., "A Hierarchy of Competencies for Teachers of Emotionally Handicapped Children." *Exceptional Children*, Vol. 33, No. 1 (September, 1966), pp. 7–11.
Hewitt, L. E., and Jenkins, Richard L., "Fundamental Patterns of Maladjustment: The Dynamics of Their Origin." Springfield, Ill., Michigan Child Guidance Institute, 1946.
Humphrey, George, "The Problem of Generalization." *Bulletin of Canadian Psychological Association*, Vol. 4, No. 3 (October, 1944), pp. 37–51.
Jacobson, Stanley, and Faegre, Christopher, "Neutralization: A Tool for the Teacher of Disturbed Children." *Exceptional Children*, 25: 243–46 (February, 1959).
Johnson, Doris J., and Myklebust, Helmer R., *Learning Disabilities: Educational Principles and Practices*. New York, Grune & Stratton, 1967.
Johnson, John L., "Teacher Preparation for Educating the Disturbed: Graduate, Undergraduate, or Functional?" *Exceptional Children*, Vol. 34, No. 5 (January, 1968), pp. 345–51.
Johnson, G. Orville, *Education for the Slow Learner*. Englewood Cliffs, N.J., Prentice-Hall, 1963.
Jordan, Thomas E., *The Exceptional Child*. Columbus, Ohio, Charles E. Merrill, 1962.

Kanner, Leo, *Child Psychiatry*. Springfield, Ill., Charles C. Thomas, 1966.

Kanner, Leo, and Eisenberg, Leon, "Notes on the Follow-up Studies of Autistic Children," in Paul H. Hoch and Joseph Zubin, eds., *Psychopathology of Childhood*. New York, Grune & Stratton, 1955, pp. 227–39.

Kirk, Samuel A., *Educating Exceptional Children*. Boston, Houghton Mifflin, 1962.

Kirk, Samuel A., *Public School Provisions for the Severely Retarded Children*. Special Report to the New York State Interdepartmental Health Resources Board. Albany, N.Y., July, 1957.

Kirk, Samuel A., "Basic Fact and Principles Underlying Special Education," in *The Education of Exceptional Children*. National Society for the Study of Education, Forty-Ninth Yearbook, Part II. Chicago, University of Chicago Press, 1950.

Kluckhohn, Clyde, *Mirror for Man*. New York, McGraw-Hill (Premier Book), 1944.

Knickerbocker, Major Barbara M., "The Significance of Body Schema and Body Image in Perceptual Motor Dysfunction," in *Proceedings: Ohio Occupational Therapy Association 1966 Conference: Body Image*. Cleveland, Ohio, 1966.

Kough, Jack, and De Haan, Robert F., *Helping Students with Special Needs*. Chicago, Science Research Associates, 1957.

Kough, Jack, and De Haan, Robert F., *Identifying Children with Special Needs*, Vol. I. Chicago, Science Research Associates, 1955.

Kreuter, Mortimer, "A Public School in a Correctional Institution." *Federal Probation*, September, 1965, pp. 50–57.

Krippner, Stanley, "Sociopathic Tendencies and Reading Retardation in Children." *Exceptional Children*, 29: 258–66 (February, 1963).

Krugman, Morris, "Appraisal and Treatment of Personality Problems in a Guidance Program," in *Education in a Free World*. Washington, D.C., American Council on Education, 1954, pp. 114–21.

Krupp, George R., and Schwartzberg, Bernard, "The Brain-Injured Child: A Challenge to Social Workers." *Social Casework*, 41: 63–69 (February, 1960).

Lamm, L. B., and Folsom, J. C., "Attitude Therapy and the Team Approach." *The Journal of Hospital and Community Psychiatry*, November, 1965, pp. 307–20.

Landis, Carney, and Bolles, M. Marjorie, *Textbook of Abnormal Psychology*. New York, Macmillan, 1947.

Larrick, Nancy, "The All-White World of Children's Books," *Saturday Review*, September 11, 1965.

Laufer, Maurice, "Emotionally Disturbed and Brain-Injured Children's Problems of Education." *Canadian Mental Health*, Vol. 14, No. 4 (1966), pp. 21–23.

Laufer, Maurice W., Denhoff, Eric, and Solomons, Gerald, "Hyperkinetic

Impulse Disorder in Children's Behavior Problems." *Psychosomatic Medicine,* Vol. 19 (January, 1957), pp. 45–46.

Lent, John E., "Helping Stutterers in the Classroom," in James F. Magary and John R. Eichorn, eds., *The Exceptional Child: A Book of Readings.* New York, Holt, Rinehart & Winston, 1962, pp. 327–29.

Long, Nicholas J., and Newman, Ruth A., "The Teacher and His Mental Health," in Nicholas J. Long, William C. Morse, and Ruth G. Newman, eds., *Conflict in the Classroom: The Education of Emotionally Disturbed Children.* Belmont, Calif., Wadsworth, 1966.

Long, Nicholas J., Morse, William C., and Newman, Ruth G., *Conflict in the Classroom: The Education of Emotionally Disturbed Children.* Belmont, Calif., Wadsworth, 1966.

Mase, Darrel J., "Emotionally Insecure and Disturbed Children," in James F. Magary and John R. Eichorn, eds., *The Exceptional Child: A Book of Readings.* New York, Holt, Rinehart & Winston, 1962, pp. 340–45.

Millender, Dharatula, M., "Selecting Our Children's Books: Time for Some Changes." *Changing Education: A Journal of the American Federation of Teachers,* Fall, 1966, pp. 8–14.

Morse, William C., "The Crisis Teacher," in Nicholas J. Long, William C. Morse, and Ruth G. Newman, eds., *Conflict in the Classroom.* Belmont, Calif., Wadsworth, 1966, pp. 251–54.

Morse, William C., "The Education of Socially Maladjusted and Emotionally Disturbed Children," in William M. Cruickshank and G. Orville Johnson, eds., *Education of Exceptional Children and Youth.* Englewood Cliffs, N.J., Prentice-Hall, 1958, pp. 557–608.

Myklebust, Helmer, *Auditory Disorders in Children.* New York, Grune & Stratton, 1954.

National Society for the Study of Education, *Forty Ninth Yearbook,* Part II. Chicago, University of Chicago Press, 1950.

New York City Board of Education, *Guidance of Children in Elementary Schools.* Curriculum Bulletin Number 13, 1955–1956 series.

Pate, John E., "Emotionally Disturbed and Socially Maladjusted Children," in Lloyd M. Dunn, ed., *Exceptional Children in the Schools.* New York, Holt, Rinehart & Winston, 1963, pp. 239–84.

Pelone, Anthony J., "The Adjustment of the Partially Seeing Child in the Regular Classroom," in James F. Magary and John R. Eichorn, eds., *The Exceptional Child: A Book of Readings.* New York, Holt, Rinehart & Winston, 1962.

Peter, Laurence J., *Prescriptive Teaching.* New York, McGraw-Hill, 1965.

Ratchik, Irving, and Koenig, Frances G., *Guidance and the Physically Handicapped Child.* Chicago, Science Research Associates, 1963.

Redl, Fritz, and Wineman, David, *The Aggressive Child.* New York, The Free Press, 1957.

Rhodes, William C., "The Disturbing Child: A Problem of Ecological Management." *Exceptional Children,* 33: 7 (March, 1967), pp. 449–55.

Rhodes, William C., "Curriculum and Disordered Behavior," in Nicholas J. Long, William C. Morse, and Ruth G. Newman, eds., *Conflict in the Classroom*. Belmont, Calif., Wadsworth, 1966, pp. 405–10.
Riessman, Frank, *The Culturally Deprived Child*. New York, Harper & Row, 1962.
Rimmele, Polly Ann, *Step by Step*. La Salle, Ill., United Cerebral Palsy Associations, 1967.
Roach, Robert E., "The Meaning of Severe Deafness in the Life of a Young Child," in James F. Magary and John R. Eichorn, eds., *The Exceptional Child: A Book of Readings*. New York, Holt, Rinehart & Winston, 1962, pp. 294–303.
Robison, Sophia M., *Juvenile Delinquency: Its Nature and Control*. New York, Holt, Rinehart & Winston, 1964.
Rosen, Irving M., "Development of Body Image," in *Proceedings: Ohio Occupational Therapy Association 1966 Conference: Body Image*. Cleveland, Ohio, 1966.
Rosenberg, Sheldon, "Problem Solving and Conceptual Behavior," in Norman R. Ellis, ed., *Handbook of Mental Deficiency: Psychological Theory and Research*. New York, McGraw-Hill, 1963, pp. 439–59.
Sarason, Seymour B., *Psychological Problems in Mental Deficiency*. New York, Harper & Brothers, 1959.
Shattuck, Marquis, "Segregation versus Non-Segregation of Exceptional Children." *Journal of Exceptional Children*, 12: 235–40 (May, 1946).
Siegel, Ernest, "Learning Disabilities: Substance or Shadow." *Exceptional Children*, Vol. 34, No. 6 (February, 1968), pp. 433–37.
Siegel, Ernest, "Some Suggestions for Developing Effective Lessons." Mimeographed paper distributed in in-service training course, The Adams School, 248 E. 31 St., New York City, 1967.
Siegel, Ernest, "Integrating Handicapped Children and Youth into Regular Religious Educational Programs." *Religious Education*, Vol. LXII, No. 4 (July–August, 1967), pp. 355–57.
Siegel, Ernest, "Special Education and Human Relations." *Digest of Mentally Retarded*, Vol. 3, No. 1 (Fall, 1966).
Siegel, Ernest, *A Comparison of Minimally Brain-Injured Children of Normal Intelligence with Non-Handicapped Children in Tactual Discrimination Abilities*, unpublished Ed. D. Dissertation. New York, Teachers College, Columbia University, 1966.
Siegel, Ernest, Gisonti, Frank, and Posnack, Gerald, *Who Said It?: A Teaching Aid in Communication*. Freeport, N.Y., Educational Activities, 1965.
Siegel, Ernest, *Helping the Brain Injured Child*. New York, New York Association for Brain Injured Children, 1961.
Skeels, Harold M., as quoted in "Environment Important." *Science News*, Vol. 90, No. 1 (October, 1966), p. 248.
Strauss, Alfred A., and Kephart, Newell C., *Psychopathology and Educa-*

Bibliography

tion of the Brain-Injured Child, Vol. II. New York, Grune & Stratton, 1955.

Strauss, Alfred A., and Lehtinen, Laura E., *Psychopathology and Education of the Brain-Injured Child,* Vol. I. New York, Grune & Stratton, 1947.

Streng, Alice, "The Child Who Is Hard of Hearing," in James F. Magary and John R. Eichorn, eds., *The Exceptional Child: A Book of Readings.* New York, Holt, Rinehart & Winston, 1962.

Stullken, Edward H., "Special Schools and Classes for the Socially Maladjusted," in *The Education of Exceptional Children.* National Society for the Study of Education, Forty-ninth Yearbook, Part II. Chicago, University of Chicago Press, 1950.

Taft, Lawrence T., "Brain-Injury—Its Definition, Diagnosis, Cause and Treatment." New York, New York Association for Brain Injured Children, n.d.

Tenny, John W., and Lennox, Margaret A., "Children with Epilepsy," in James F. Magary and John R. Eichorn, eds., *The Exceptional Child: A Book of Readings.* New York, Holt, Rinehart & Winston, 1962.

Thelander, H. E., Phelps, Jane K., and Kirk, E. Walton, "Learning Disabilities Associated with Lesser Brain Damage." *Journal of Pediatrics,* Vol. 53, No. 4 (October, 1958), pp. 405–409.

Treatman, Paul, *Teacher's License Training Text: Assistant-to-Principal, Junior Principal, and Principal.* New York, Arco, 1957.

Tregold, A. F., *A Textbook of Mental Deficiency.* New York, William Wood & Co., 1937.

Ullmann, Leonard B., and Krasner, Leonard, *Case Studies in Behavior Modifications.* New York, Holt, Rinehart & Winston, 1965.

U.S. Office of Education Bulletin No. 11 "Teachers of Children Who Are Socially and Emotionally Maladjusted," prepared by Romaine Mackie, William C. Kvaraceus, and Harold Williams, 1957.

Voelker, Paul H., "Administration and Supervision of Special Education Programs," in William M. Cruickshank and Orville G. Johnson, eds., *Education of Exceptional Children and Youth.* Englewood Cliffs, N.J., Prentice-Hall, 1958, pp. 648–98.

Waleski, Dorothy, "The Physically Handicapped in the Classroom." *NEA Journal,* Vol. 53, No. 9 (December, 1964), pp. 12–16.

Walsh, John F., and O'Connor, Sister James Dolores, "When Are Children Disturbed?" *The Elementary School Journal,* April, 1968, pp. 353–56.

Webster's New Twentieth Century Dictionary of the English Language—Unabridged. New York, Standard Reference Works Publishing Co., 1956.

Wechsler, David, "The IQ Is an Intelligent Test." *The New York Times Magazine,* June 26, 1966.

Wolfensberger, Wolf, "Embarrassments in the Diagnostic Process." *Mental*

Retardation (published by the American Association on Mental Deficiency), Vol. 3, No. 3 (June, 1965), pp. 29–31.

Woltman, Adolph G., "The Use of Puppetry in Therapy," in Nicholas J. Long, William C. Morse, and Ruth G. Newman, eds., *Conflict in the Classroom*. Belmont, Calif., Wadsworth, 1966, pp. 202–208.

Wooden, Harley Z., "What Is Special About Special Education: The Child Who Is Deaf." *Exceptional Children,* 19: 179–82 (February, 1953).

Wright, Beatrice A., *Physical Disability—A Psychological Approach*. New York, Harper & Brothers, 1960.

Young, Milton A., *Teaching Children with Special Learning Needs: A Problem-Solving Approach,* New York, John Day, 1967.

Zeaman, David, and House, Betty J., "The Role of Attention in Retardate Discrimination Learning," in Norman J. Ellis, ed., *Handbook of Mental Deficiency: Psychological Theory and Research*. New York, McGraw-Hill, 1963.

Index

Abstract thinking
  activities for improving, 77–83
  aspects of, 75–77
  difficulties in, 76–77
  special learning principles for improving, 83

Aggressiveness
  in brain-injured child, 25, 27
  in socially maladjusted child, 31, 35–38
  suggestions for reducing, 87–93

Ancillary services
  guidance programs, 133–35
  utilized by school administrator, 132–35

Animism, in brain-injured child, 24–25

Anxiety
  as a cause of communication disorder, 96–98
  in brain-injured children, 26
  in exceptional children, 50–51
  negative cycles of, 51
  suggestions for reducing, 51–55

Attentiveness
  activities for improving, 56–63
  difficulty for brain-injured child, 20–21, 55, 56, 97
  difficulty for culturally deprived, 55–56
  difficulty for emotionally disturbed child, 55
  difficulty for mentally retarded child, 55

Awkwardness. *See* Poor Coordination

Behavior problems
  definition, 84
  in brain-injured child, 20, 24, 25, 84
  in emotionally disturbed child, 30–31, 84–85
  in mentally retarded child, 19, 84
  suggestions for diminishing, 85–92
Body image
  activities for developing, 72–74
  problems in brain-injured child, 72–73
  problems in emotionally disturbed child, 73
Brain-injured
  characteristics, 20–28
  definition, 19–20
  overlapping, 32
  prevalence, 14
  prognosis for, 28

"Calendar Curriculum," 60–61
Communication. *See also* Language skills
  developing skills in, 98–101
  relation to social maturity, 97–98
  teacher's verbalisms, 56–57, 89–90
Community
  attitudes of, 140
  as a resource, 139–40
  and school administrator, 139–42
  and teacher-training institutions, 149–51
Conceptualizing. *See* Abstract thinking
Concrete materials, and aid in conceptualizing, 77–78
Conferences and conventions
  teacher's role in, 116
  teacher-training institutions' role in, 150
Consistency, in preventing undesirable behavior, 88–89
Copying written materials
  difficulties in, 65–66
  remediation, 66–68
Crisis teacher, role of, 130
Culturally deprived
  experiences in listening, 58, 90
  inattention in, 55–56
  in relation to mentally retarded, 16
  time sense in, 60–61
  use of games in educating, 61–62

Index

Delinquent behavior
  in mentally retarded, 19
  in socially maladjusted, 31, 35–38
Destructiveness, in brain-injured child, 24
Diagnosis
  difficulties of, 6–8
  early, 8
  inadequate, 7
  misdiagnosis, 7
  nondiagnosis, 7
  in relation to teacher attitudes, 47
  teacher's role in, 108–11
Disorganization
  problems caused by, 63
  in relation to handwriting difficulty, 67–68
  suggestions for diminishing, 64–65
Distractibility. *See also* Attentiveness
  as cause of communication problems, 97
  in brain-injured child, 21
  used to child's advantage, 90

Early identification, teacher's role in, 108–9
Egocentric thinking
  as cause of communication problems, 97
  in mentally retarded children, 53–54

Emotional disturbance
  amelioration of, 38–40
  behavior deviation, 30
  caused by other handicapping conditions, 13–14
  characteristics
    neurotic, 34
    psychopathic personality, 34
    psychosomatic disorders, 34
    psychotic, 33–34
    school phobic, 34
  coping mechanisms of, 36–37
  definition, 28–33
  etiology, 36–38
  general characteristics, 34–35
  institutionalization of, 37
  overlapping, 32
  prevalence, 14
  psychotic, 28, 29
  socially maladjusted, 30–31
Exceptional children, definition, 2–4, 13

Failure-free activities, for anxious child, 51
Fatigability, in anxious child, 52

Games
  used in listening training, 59–60

used to improve coordination, 69, 73–75
used to increase attentiveness, 61–62
used to promote socialization skills, 96, 102
used to reduce anxiety, 54
used to strengthen conceptualization, 82
Guidance
establishing school programs in, 133–35
of teacher trainees, 149
Guilelessness, in brain-injured child, 25

Handwriting. *See* Copying written materials
Home-school-community relations, on university level, 149–50. *See also* Teacher-parent relations
Humor
used in good mental hygiene approach, 92
used to offset anxiety, 54
Hyperactivity, in brain-injured child, 21

Impulsiveness
as cause of communication problems, 97
in brain-injured child, 21–22
Independent activities
as part of lesson, 121
training for, 91–92
Information gathering
purposes, 112
techniques and instruments for, 112–13
In-service training
conferences and conventions, 116–17
in developing teacher attitudes, 117–19
participation in, 116–19
role of school administrator, 128–30
Institutionalization of emotionally disturbed, 37
Interest of child, related to attention, 60–61
Irritability, in brain-injured child, 22–23
Itinerant teacher, 130, 136

Language skills, activities for improving, 98–101
Lesson, the
as aid in maintaining good behavior, 93
suggestions for increasing effectiveness of, 120–21
variety of activities in, 57, 121

Index

Lesson planning, and significance for exceptional children, 119
Listening
  as socialization skill, 94
  training for, 59–60

Maladaptive behavior, learned, 48–49
Materials
  classroom distribution, 56
  concrete, 77–78
  relating to child's interests, 60–61
  suitable to chronological age, 61
Mental hygiene approach. *See also* Teacher attitudes
  pride in appearance, 92
  to improve self-concept, 92–93
  to reduce disorganization, 65
  use of direct appeal to child, 93
  use of humor, 92
  use of praise, 48–49
Mentally retarded
  characteristics, 17–19
    educable, 17
    overlapping, 32
    secondary, 18
    trainable, 18–19
  classification, 16–17
  definition, 15–16
  prevalence, 14
  prognosis for, 15–16
  special principles for education, 83
Misdiagnosis, 7

Neurotic, characteristics of, 34
Nondiagnosis, 7, 8

Older children
  coordination and body image activities, 70, 74
  language skills activities, 82
  listening training activities, 59–60
  relating with younger children, 55, 102
One-to-one teaching, need for experience in, 146
Overinhibited children, 33, 35, 37

Parent organizations
  administrator's role in, 135, 140
  teacher's role in, 125–26
  teacher-training personnel's role in, 150
Parent-teacher relations. *See* Relationship between parents and teachers
Perseveration
  as cause of communication problems, 97

in brain-injured child, 22
used to child's advantage, 90–91
Physical movement, providing for, 58–59
Placement
administrator's role in, 136
of exceptional children in regular class, 1–5, 94, 129
"Planned ignoring," used to prevent undesirable behavior, 89
Poor coordination
activities for remediating, 68–75
causes, 68, 70, 72–73
in brain-injured child, 23, 68
in mentally retarded child, 18
in emotionally disturbed child, 68
Poor self-concept
as cause of maladaptive behavior, 31, 96–97
in mentally retarded child, 18
teacher's role in changing, 46–50
Poor speech, in brain-injured child, 23–24
Prevalence
brain-injured, 14
emotionally disturbed, 14
mentally retarded, 14
slow learner, 14
Private tutoring, as supportive service, 114, 132–33
Program modifications, examples of, 137–38
Proximity control, used to prevent undesirable behavior, 87–88
Psychopathic personality, characteristics of, 34
Psychosomatic disorders, characteristics of, 34
Psychotherapy, as supportive service, 113–14
Psychotic, characteristics of, 33–34
Puppetry, as teaching technique in reducing anxiety, 53

Record keeping
as aid to teaching, 112
as corollary of lesson planning, 121
by guidance personnel, 133–34
in junior high and high schools, 133, 138–39
Referrals, by teachers, 109, 114–15
Relationship between parents and teacher

Index

establishing positive attitudes in, 124
to improve child's coordination, 75
need to communicate, 122–23, 135
negative attitudes in, 122
to reduce child's disorganization, 64
Role of school administrator
in evaluating programs, 138–39
in home-school relations, 135
in making program modifications, 137–38
in obtaining teaching materials, 136–37
in placement, 136
in working with community, 139–42
support of child, 129–32
support of teacher, 132–36
teacher recruitment, 131–32
Routines, 85–87

"Scatter," in brain-injured child, 27
School phobic
etiology, 34
program modifications for, 138
Self-preoccupation, teaching techniques to diminish, 53–55

Semantic problem
in defining "brain injury," 19–20
in defining "emotionally disturbed," 28–29
Sensory deprivation
effects of, 5
partial, 5–6
related to physical movement, 58–59
Sequential approach
in developing socialization skills, 102–3
in improving coordination, 68–70, 74
in improving handwriting, 66–67
in increasing conceptualization skills, 83
in listening training, 60
"Signal interference," used to prevent undesirable behavior, 87
"Snowballing," prevention of, 87
Social immaturity
in brain-injured child, 25–26, 92–93
in emotionally disturbed, 92–93
in mentally retarded, 92–93
related to communication ability, 97–101

suggestions for reducing, 94–103
Socialized aggressive children, 33, 35, 37. *See also* Delinquent behavior
Socially maladjusted
 characteristics, 35–38
 definition, 30–31
 etiology, 36–38
 overinhibited, 33, 35, 37
 socialized aggressive, 33, 35, 37
 unsocialized aggressive, 33, 35, 37
Special education
 courses in, 144–46
 definition, 1–4
Speech therapy, for mildly handicapped, 113
Stimuli reduction, 56
Success assured activities
 in improving behavior, 92
 in improving self-image, 47
 in reducing anxiety, 51
Supportive services
 need for, 114, 115
 private tutoring, 114
 psychotherapist, 113–14
 speech teachers, 113
 visual-training specialists, 114

Talkativeness, in brain-injured child, 23

Teacher attitudes
 in ameliorating emotional disturbance, 38–40
 developed via teacher-training research programs, 151
 in relation to child's self-concept, 46–47
 in relation to disorganization and handwriting difficulty, 67–68
 role of in-service training in, 116–19, 143–46
Teacher competencies
 as key to teacher selection, 131
 of teacher trainees, 148–49
 at university level, 147
Teacher recruitment, administrator's role in, 131–32
Teacher-training institution
 developing research projects, 150–51
 selection of teacher trainees, 148–49
 suggested teacher preparation modifications, 143–49
 working with community, 149–50

Unit method
 in promoting socialization, 95

Index

in reducing inattentiveness, 63

Unsocialized aggressive children, 33, 35, 37

Value judgments, avoidance of, 49

Variety of activities, need for, 57, 121

Visual perceptual training
to improve poor coordination, 71–72
problems relating to learning difficulties, 72
as supportive service, 114

Withdrawn child, 36–37, 58